# RELATIONSHIP COMMUNICATION

*How to Resolve Any Conflict With Your Partner, Avoid
Communication Mistakes, Create Deeper Intimacy, and
Gain Healthy Conflict Resolution in Your Relationship*

**Emily Richards**

# TABLE OF CONTENTS

# INTRODUCTION

Thank you very much for purchasing *Relationship Communication*. I sincerely appreciate that you have done so. With this book, my mission is to help you and your partner form the deepest and most trusting bond that you can in your relationship endeavors. I wish to do this by giving you advice on relationship communication, as it is the glue that holds all stable relationships together. That is what we want. Stability is critical for the foundation of any relationship, lest it crumbles and falls apart before you have the chance to build it up. I hope beyond hope that my book helps accomplish and tackle, in part, some of the obstacles that you may come across in your relationship endeavors. Together, we can grow, learn, overcome obstacles, and resolve conflicts. I want this book to be a guiding light that will help you navigate those waters. I hope that I have accomplished that task sufficiently.

Throughout this book, we will cover, in a series of chapters and subchapters, many topics revolving around relationship communication. We will be going over what relationship communication is, what it means, and how it pertains to your life. I will also go over the different forms of communication that we can use, such as verbal, signed, written, body language, and communication through physical touch. Then, we will move on to conflict resolution and the steps involved to overcome it in the best possible way. We will go over ways to avoid conflict, methods of treading the waters of conflict calmly and constructively, and things to be avoided in a conflict.

After all of that is discussed, we will go into the most common relationship communication mistakes that people make, as well as how to resolve them. We will further that resolve by discussing empathy and its positive impact on our relationships and emotional health.

Then comes the steamy subject: Intimacy. Yes, believe it or not, communication plays a big and constructive role in heating things up in the bedroom. From passionate discussions to borders and expectations to making one another feel appreciated, communication is as intertwined as the two of you will be after reading the chapter.

To wrap it all up, we will recap on healthy conflict resolution, as it is a big subject in many budding *and* developed relationships, and then we will finish it off with a nice discussion about how to talk about difficult subjects in a trusting and comforting relationship environment as well as what the five languages of love are and how to identify and incorporate them into your relationships.

Though there are many relationship books on the market today, I am grateful that you have chosen this one. I made sure to fill it with the most enriching, honest, and helpful information on the subject matter that is available today. I hope that this book enlightens you and strengthens your relationship, and I wish you the best in the days to come. I sincerely believe that if you follow the advice in this book, your relationship will be much more open, strong, and fulfilling for both you and your partner. I hope you enjoy it!

# CHAPTER 1
## *The Basics: What Is Relationship Communication?*

To begin, let us answer the most basic question that is posed when one picks up this book: What is relationship communication? How we define this concept will shape our understanding of the chapters to come and solidify the hoops we must jump through to gain the most peaceful, intimate, durable, and loving bond that we can with our partner.

## What Relationship Communication Means

Relationship communications, in the simplest terms, is exactly what it sounds like. It is the communication between individuals who are in a relationship, but what does that mean? Proper relationship communication is imperative to keeping a relationship healthy because it allows that relationship to be open, honest, and non-secretive.

There is no way in our common realm of understanding to read a person's mind. Therefore, to know your partner's needs and wants, or to communicate your own needs and wants to them, you must be able to relay that information. That is why healthy relationship communication is a must. Without it, anger, confusion, frustration, and distrust have a nasty habit of seeping into a relationship.

At its very core, you can say that relationship communication is all about proper connections and pathways for the open and honest transfer of basic needs, thoughts, feelings, wants, and ideas in a relationship. It is a deep conversation that goes past the daily small talk that we all engage in, and it reaches the root of feelings and views on life itself and daily obstacles. A good starting point in any relationship is to let your partner know that you care, that you are there to listen, and to both have an open dialogue about your personalities, short and long-term goals, morals, and more that will pertain to your lives and your relationship together.

It's also good to let your partner know that you are there for them and that you can quietly sit and listen to what they have to say engagingly. Let them know that you are their number one fan, support system, and confidant, and hopefully, they can do the same for you. Get into each other's heads through proper, deep dialogue and learn to understand each other's point of view so you can avoid conflict down the road. We will talk more about that later. For now, we will delve deeper into what it means to communicate and how relationship communication works.

## How Does Relationship Communication Work?

Now that we know what relationship communication is, how does it work? Well, it means that you need to put in the effort to properly communicate your thoughts, needs, wants, etc. with your partner. This can be through body language, spoken words, written words and images, and physical acts. We will go over each of these communication outlets here to further your understanding of how each works and how you can apply them to your relationship moving forward.

## Body Language

Many people don't notice body language concerning communication, but it is incredibly critical, whether obviously or subtly, to one's understanding of the message that their partner gives off or is trying to give off. Body language can be as small as folding one's hands together or as big as knitted eyebrows and an angry frown. It all coincides with communication.

Body language is one of the unspoken forms of communication that we often miss unless it's blatantly obvious, such as a frown, wink, or smile. It is a great indication of emotion, and it is a very intimate way to know someone by being able to read their body to tell how they are feeling. It will greatly strengthen your relationship and your communication capabilities once you and your partner learn how to read each other's bodies.

Once you can read the body language of your partner, and not confuse it as this can lead to relationship stumbles and obstacles, it will be incredibly beneficial for you both. It is also very intimate and can make you and your partner feel much closer when just a passing glance lets you know how they are feeling.

With that in mind, it is important to pay attention to your body language so that you do not give off the wrong impression from day to day. For example, when you are sitting with your partner, take care to avoid crossing your arms or legs, for that makes you seem distant, disinterested in their company or conversation or uncomfortable. If it is comfortable for you to sit this way, convey that to your partner, so they do not feel offended or get the wrong idea in a situation such as this.

Rolling your eyes is another negative form of body language and expression. It is snarky, disrespectful in most cases, and hurtful if you are not joking. If you are joking, make sure to voice that and make sure you can read positive body language in your partner. If your partner stiffens, frowns, or slumps their shoulders, it is an indication that you may need to apologize and clarify the situation. Always follow up an action or an ambiguous form of body language with a verbal affirmation of what you have done so that your partner does not get the wrong idea.

Try to be as open as you can with your body language, so the atmosphere is warmer and more inviting. This will keep away negative energies and emotions on a more subtle level, pushing away the possibility for further complications down the road.

Maintaining eye contact is also very important because whether you believe so or not, it shows that you are truly listening to what your partner is saying. If you speak or listen when looking away from your partner, you may seem distant or disinterested in the conversation, or your partner.

With all of that said, it is easy to see that body language is an important first step to recognizing the basics of communication in your relationship! Maintain positive body language throughout your relationship, so your partner always feels appreciated. It will be the detriment of the relationship if you are not consistent because if you start out strong and then let it all fade over time, the relationship will crumble. Something as simple as a smile can work wonders even if you don't realize it.

Examples of body language communication, direct or indirect, include:
- Crossed arms during a conversation or argument, symbolizing closing oneself off to the conversation and being angry, upset, or confrontational, or putting up proverbial walls
- A blush, meaning embarrassment, a flush of passion, nervousness, fear, or another strong but subsidiary emotion
- Tapping one's foot or fingers, symbolizing nervousness or impatience
- A smile, frown, knitted brows, or other facial cues
- Opening your arms out wide as an indication that you would like to embrace

## Spoken Words

The act of speaking words, or using sign language for the hearing impaired, is the most common and easily identifiable form of communication that we know of today. It is direct, easily understood, and telling. Therefore, it is easy to utilize speech for dialogue between two romantic partners. However, it is also easy to wield as a weapon, so one must be careful with this form of communication as well.

Speaking our thoughts, feelings, ideas, and desires is critical for fostering a healthy relationship between two people. When you voice a problem, it can be resolved. When you tell your partner that you care about them, it is heartwarming and strengthens the relationship.

Words are powerful. Yes, actions speak louder than words, but the words are the stepping stone for further action. Use your words to the advantage of your relationship and strive to be open, honest, expressive, and affectionate. This is a wonderful way to get a good foundation started for your relationship.

When you have an argument, you speak. When you tell your partner "I love you" for the first time, you often speak those words. Words are so incredibly intertwined into any relationship that this is not an area that can be skipped over. Use your words very carefully, and think every sentence through before you speak it. You can apologize all you want, but you can never take back the words you say, no matter how hard you try. Always speak thoughtfully, caringly, and honestly.

I cannot stress this point enough because it is imperative going forward in this book and in the life of your relationship as a whole. Make sure you are intentional and careful with your words, and it will go a long way.

Examples of spoken word communication include:

- A phone call
- Speaking directly, person to person
- A voicemail
- A song
- A question or query
- A compliment
- Words of affirmation
- Verbal criticism

## Written Words and Images/Media Communication

In this day and age, this section might as well be called texting, but as I know that there is more to written words than that, I will leave the section titled as is. I want to hope and believe that couples still leave sweet written notes and messages for their partner. Therefore, I will put that as an example of the personal touch of communication in this section as well.

With that clarified, I will say that written word communication is just about on par with spoken these days. With the amount of texting and instant messaging that we do every day, it is nearly taking over our overall communication. With that said, you must take a lot of care when you communicate with your partner.

The good thing is that it is a lot easier to think about what you type or write before you send it. You can erase, backspace, and rewrite instead of blurting out words verbally that you cannot take back. That is an advantage. The disadvantage is that we often send messages very quickly without truly thinking them through or proofreading them. Try not to get into this habit.

Another concern with written communication is that emotions do not translate well through text, even with pictures or emojis. Make sure to write eloquently enough to get your point across while avoiding dialogue that could be construed as vague, harsh, blunt, or sarcastic. Make sure to back up your words with verbal communication, as well, when you have the change so that miscommunication and confusion do not occur. This is imperative if you want to maintain healthy communication in a relationship. People find their meanings and jump to conclusions when reading things quite often, so it is best to make sure that you accurately convey your message.

Examples of written word or image communication include:

- Emails
- Texts
- Emojis
- Instant messages
- Handwritten notes, such as a small note slipped into a lunch bag, a sticky note on the window, or a message on the mirror
- Magnets rearranged on the refrigerator
- A steamy note on the bathroom mirror made from the condensation
- A small picture indicating love or some other emotion
- A painting
- A greeting card
- A funny video

## Physical Acts

Much like body language, physical acts are a great nonverbal way to communicate your feelings and intentions through touch. This is likely the most intimate of the forms of communication I will be covering in this chapter. It is more direct than body language as well, so it is easier to convey your intentions in this manner. However, try to follow up on your physical actions with verbal dialogue to make sure consent is agreed upon, and messages are conveyed correctly.

There are obvious and ambiguous forms of physical communication, and it is important to note that difference. Obvious forms of physical communication include crying, which is most often associated with either sadness or joy. It's easy to notice if someone is crying with sadness, as they will likely frown or slump their shoulders. If they are crying with joy, it is likely accompanied by bright eyes and a smile. You can always follow up on these actions with words for further clarity. If your partner is crying, make sure to ask if your partner is ok and offer comfort in either of the two situations I have mentioned here.

A more ambiguous form of physical communication, and one that needs a bit of verbal affirmation and consent, could be something along the lines of a kiss or the action of placing your hand on your partner's leg. You need to back these up with spoken communication in order to assess your partner's reaction and convey your intentions. For example, if you place your hand on your partner's leg, it could be an invitation for intimacy or a simple caress of comfort. Verbally express your intentions while asking if your partner is ok with the acts involved. This second layer of communication will help you both remain comfortable and will eliminate an awkward moment of confusion.

Make sure to curb your more aggressive physical communication, such as grabbing your partner forcefully by the arm, getting in their face during an argument, or pushing them away. This can lead to many negative outcomes down the road. Try to replace that aggression with thoughtful words and honest concerns that are spoken calmly.

On the flip side, try to express warm emotions and feelings more frequently, such as warm hugs, sweet kisses, hand holding, and more to let your partner know that you are there, you care, and you want to be near them. Even the little things show how much you appreciate your partner, such as when you brush the hair from your partner's face, lay your head on your partner's shoulder, or simply sit next to your partner when you watch a movie. Try not to distance yourself too much, and always let your partner know that you are there, with proper boundaries if necessary.

Examples of indirect or direct physical communication include:

- Crying as an open and direct communication of sadness, anger, or frustration
- Laying your head on your partner's shoulders and/or wrapping your arms around them to show you need their support, love, affection, touch, etc.
- Placing a hand on your partner's leg, indicating a want for physical touch for comfort or intimacy
- Kissing your partner on the cheek to show you care for them but aren't necessarily initiating sexual intimacy
- When you place a hand on your partner's shoulder to show that you are listening and that you are there. It is a connective gesture that can strengthen your relationship, similar to holding hands.

## How Respect and Trust Tie into Healthy Relationship Communication

Almost as important, if not more important, than proper dialogue in a relationship is respect and trust. These tie into the stability of the relationship and hold it together like glue. Communication ties right into that steadfastness as your words and actions dictate your ability to trust, receive trust, respect, and receive respect. Your words and actions can either hold your relationship together or cause it to crumble and fall apart, just like trust and respect can.

Always, always back up your words with proper actions and stay consistent with what you say and do. If you tell your partner that you love them, back it up with words of affirmation, affection, physical touch if they are comfortable with that, fidelity, and respect for your partner and their things. If you say you will do something, do it. If you say you won't do something, don't do it. If you tell them something, back it up with an action that affirms your words. It's all in the consistency, which we will cover soon.

Respect is important, for if you do not respect each other you will never truly listen to or acknowledge what one another says. Furthermore, never belittle your partner with your words. Just as your words can lift up and support your partner in a cocoon of love, they can cut like a sharp knife and cut away the happiness and security of your relationship. Words are powerful, and they are critical for maintaining proper respect in a relationship. Make sure your partner always knows that you appreciate what they do, and follow up any positive action with words of affirmation! It will make your partner feel special, and it will foster the reciprocation of respect and positive reinforcement in the relationship.

Contempt and condescension are detrimental to a relationship, and these are the opposite of respect. Keep them at bay, and if your partner does not do something you like, instead of speaking down, lift them up with encouragement and constructive criticism. Meet your partner at their level, and never look down upon them. This is destructive and damaging, will lower your partner's self-esteem, and will make your partner feel unloved and unappreciated.

Just remember this: The closer you get to your partner, romantically, sexually, emotionally, or otherwise, the stronger your respect should be for that partner. Respect should not fade over time, for love will not grow that way. Love and respect should go hand in hand, so the deeper your relationship gets, the greater the level of respect should become. Weak levels of respect lead to a weakened relationship overall, and over time.

Now, do not confuse respect with a level of formality. You can let your guard down around your partner. Just don't be rude! Show them the same level of respect that you expect yourself. Treat your partner with kindness, care, and respect. You don't have to be rigid by any means, just practice common courtesy and let your partner know how much you appreciate what they do every day. This can be as simple as a smile, a hug, a compliment, or saying please and thank you. It does not have to be complicated or difficult by any means. Just don't harm your relationship by shutting off your connection to your partner with harsh words and disrespect. Remember, relationships should flow well and remain open and honest, but not harsh. Minimize the friction and simply be kind and courteous to the one you care for.

Trust is critical for letting your partner know that you believe what they say and that you can both make faithful promises to one another. Trust can be as simple as giving your partner the benefit of the doubt before you jump to conclusions, or it can be as intricate as believing that when they go out with friends, they will always come home to you, and you know that they have been true. You should know that you can always trust and fall back onto your partner, knowing that they will catch you and hold you up. The strength of your bond is built on a foundation of trust and honesty, and you must cherish that in order to keep that strength steadfast.

Trust builds comfort. It builds a cushion with which to fall back on when you are weary or struggling. Fill that cushion, your relationship, with the padding of accountability and dependability so neither you nor your partner will ever crash-land into rocky terrain. Hold each other up, develop a support system for each other, and stay true, always, to your words and actions. There is nothing more beneficial in a relationship than a strong foundation of trust and support. If you know you can always rely on each other, there is nothing that can bring you down.

Another way to build trust is to try new things, accomplish tasks together to build dependability, and take small risks or leaps of faith to see if you come out stronger together. Putting in an effort toward a reward together will make you both come out more fulfilled and with a tighter bond. Go on a romantic adventure together, somewhere neither of you has ever been before, and traverse its waters, overcome its obstacles, and have fun! Let your walls come down, if even for a brief period, and let loose! See if your partner can hold you up as you soar to new heights, and learn how to depend on one another with no bars held. It can be very enlightening, thrilling, and beneficial to you both as people and as a unit. Step outside your comfort zone with your partner, and maybe they will follow suit and do the same. Stretch and grow and support one another through those growing pains so you can develop both independently and together as one. This will help your relationship reach new heights, and it will feel good, too!

It is also best to maintain the ability to be trusted and respected, as well as the ability to stay sincere and stable. Always be honest, stay true to your word, keep your promises, and back up every statement with a positively reinforced action that affirms your dialogue. Stay faithful and do not waver. Keep your promises true, and do not break them without proper cause or without discussing it first with your partner. Stay open, be honest, and let your partner know ahead of time if anything is going to be changed.

A relationship is a rock that must not be moved, only grown upon and developed. It has to be stable, unshakeable, and true. If either of the individuals in a relationship shatters or move it with unfaithfulness or lies, it can wreak havoc on that relationship. The rock will crumble and fall with dishonesty and blatant disrespect of your partner. Keep this in mind going forward, and remember it before starting any new relationship or rekindling an old one.

Another good point to take note of is to be open and vulnerable. Once you are comfortable in your relationship, it's ok to let your walls down a bit so you can breathe and communicate openly. If you have been hurt in the past and are wary about opening up, a good starting point is letting your partner know that so that you don't convey a distance or a barrier that cannot be shaken.

Let your partner take you in and comfort you, and build trust together so that you can start the process of breaking down those walls. This is where true trust comes in. It may be difficult starting out, but if you maintain proper communication and faith in one another everything will turn out fine. As long as you are both open and honest, those walls will come down naturally and comfortably, I'm sure.

## Consistency and Its Important Role in Relationship Communication

As I've mentioned, one of the most important things to remember about your communication in your relationship is consistency. Consistency eliminates confusion, makes it harder to slip up and do something that will negatively impact your relationship, and allows for a common, stable ground with which your relationship can stand on.

Consistency, as it pertains to a relationship and the communication therein, can be best defined as being a cocktail of repetitive, positive behaviors that remain predictable over time. Examples of these behaviors include trust, dependability, strong desire, the need to maintain the bond with your partner, companionship, predictability, solid communication practices, and the absence of false personality or pretending to feel something that you do not.

The last point in that paragraph, regarding false feelings, is a big point that hits home regarding trust. Do not live a lie and pretend to feel a certain way when you do not honestly feel that way. It paves a foundation of dishonesty and will shatter easily over time, leading to the downfall of a relationship. It is very hard to consistently hold a lie, so try to avoid it at all costs.

Consistency also pertains to how you treat your partner. Stay consistent in how you treat your partner so that you do not catch your partner off guard or unintentionally hurt that individual. If you greet your partner a certain way every day, do not change it suddenly, or it could harm your partner's perception of the situation and cause your partner to think that your relationship has changed course without their knowledge. The communication of thoughts, intentions, and information in general within your relationship must remain consistent to avoid confusion in the short and long-term.

Consistency thoroughly ties into the previous idea of trust and dependability in a relationship. If consistency is kept, you can be relied upon more easily, and you will also have more predictable dialogue, so your partner does not have to be fearful of your reaction in certain situations. It also makes you more dependable, and it helps further reinforce the stability of your relationship.

Consistency will also make you and your partner feel more relaxed. You won't have to be on edge or walk on eggshells around your partner, because that foundation of consistency will be there. Just stay true to your character and your relationship, and don't waver regarding how you react and respond. In the end, if you heed these words, your relationship will be a hard egg to crack.

# CHAPTER 2
## *How To Resolve Any Conflict With Your Partner*

This step may seem like a bit of a tricky one, or even too good to be true, but it's not, and I will show you why. Taking the proper steps to build a good foundation for your communication in your relationship, and following the guidelines I am about to show you, will pave the way for smooth sailing in the long run. No matter what relationship storms brew, or what tries to strike the two of you down, you can weather the storm and smooth those waters with ease. The key is communication, conflict resolution, and respect.

To start, I will say that arguments, when they do not get out of hand, can actually be healthy for a relationship, contrary to popular belief. There is no perfect relationship, and if you have a relationship with no conflict, and no give and take, then there is something amiss. Either one or both are pushing down their feelings and not acknowledging issues, which is very dangerous, or they have both shut off completely and would rather ignore or avoid issues. Neither of these things is good, and it is the opposite of healthy relationship communication.

The blossoming of arguments in a relationship is actually a sign of relationship growth. It shows that both of you are comfortable enough in the relationship to let your walls down a bit and share your differences and discomforts. It is just one of the many forms of relationship communication. The catch is that it will either foster growth in your relationship or tear it down, depending on how it is handled.

Everyone is different in some way, so the views of one versus another may not jive too well in the beginning. You have to sort through that and compromise, and it all has to be out in the open in a healthy way so that you may resolve your differences positively.

If you have an issue, your partner and you have to discuss that issue, or it will never be resolved. It will just build and build and build until the lid bursts off, and it becomes an absolute, big, chaotic mess full of hurt and confusion. You have to communicate. By resolving these disagreements, in a way that is healthy and non-aggressive, it can create a deeper bond of understanding between you and your partner and bring you closer as a couple. It also breeds stability and trust, and a wonderful sense of comfort if you both know that not every disagreement will end in a sparring match.

Now, if a disagreement occurs, let's go over some various steps and guidelines for what to, and not to, do.

## Consider Each Other's Perspectives

When in an argument, make sure not to jump to conclusions prematurely. Before you speak, take a moment to consider where your partner is coming from and why. Take a moment, stop, reflect, breathe, think, and then speak. Do not attack, mind you, and do not speak from assumption. Phrase any assumptions as a question to assess your partner's point of view. Specifically, ask what is troubling your partner and why, and with the foundation of trust you have built, you can accept and believe their answer. Then build upon that answer, state your side, and calmly discuss the perspectives each of you has so you can find the root of the issue.

This is one of the most critical parts of any argument. In order to avert the attention away from the individuals and the raw emotions, you can focus on the matter at hand and attack *that* together so you can fall back onto common and stable ground. You can even dance a little jig once it is all said and done if that's something you like to do.

Basically, what I'm saying here is that you should always use empathy, trust, and intuition to assess the situation and view the world from your partner's eyes. This is not to say that you should assume what they feel right off the bat, but you can get a better picture of how they feel if you let your walls down and step into their shoes a bit. It will build trust, as well, if they know that you consider their opinion enough to take the time to feel out the situation. You will bond over it, and the issue may just resolve all on its own if you get to the root of understanding where your partner is coming from.

## Do Not Yell!

Yelling, instead of speaking in a calm tone, can make it much harder for points to get across, as the aggression will ultimately spark fear, aggression, pain, or other negative responses in the recipient of the shouting. It will just meddle the auditory reception of the words and throw a veil of disinterest over what you are saying if you start out in a screaming match. Yelling is never a good idea.

All yelling will do is get you both so fired up that you will never resolve the issue. When you feel like you are about to yell or fly off the handle, calmly excuse yourself, let your partner know that you both need to cool off, and go take some deep breaths and reflect before coming back. The key here is that you should not go back to the conversation, until you are sure that you are both calmed down.

However, do not leave the argument completely and ignore it without revisiting it. Revisit the argument that same day, after you have both calmed down, and speak calmly. Talk through each of the issues separately, try not to get off-topic or too chaotic, and make sure each of the issues is resolved before moving on to the next.

Speaking in a calm but clear voice is going to take you both so much farther than starting out a conversation with raised, high-pitched voices. It's much harder to grasp the concepts of the discussion if volumes and pitches are rising sky-high and fluctuating. The human ear picks up on these fluctuations and focuses on them, which could cause a spike in anxiety and the fight or flight response in your adrenal glands. This pitches you into a more primal mindset that can toss you into attack mode and throw the conversation way off base. So, breathe, lower your voice, and speak. Communicate with your words and not your volume and harsh tone. This is true communication, and it will ultimately resolve the problem much faster.

## Do Not Belittle Your Partner

Belittling your partner can hurt their self-esteem and cause negative friction between the both of you, opening the door for disrespect and harmful words that neither of you means but can never take back. Tread carefully here. You and your partner are supposed to be equals in your relationship. Do not let one of you dominate over the other and force submission in any situation. This can be damaging to your relationship and the self-esteem of the parties involved. Don't insight a power-struggle. Cultivate a conversation that can lead to resolution and peace.

Next, both of you should focus on self-esteem. It is an important and critical factor in any conflict resolution. It is essential to standing your ground in an argument and not wavering in your decisions, as well as maintaining good communication without getting anxious. Bolstering your self-esteem, without getting haughty, can actually build a good foundation for avoiding future disagreements.

Finally, avoid being passive-aggressive, and strive to be direct but not condescending. Passive aggression can make your partner feel belittled just because you are petty enough not to tackle the issue head-on, resorting to derogatory means that are subtle and confusing.

To recap a bit, these are the possible negative outcomes of low self-esteem that can come from belittling your partner:

- Heightened sensitivity upon taking things too personally over time, as it can lead to feelings of being attacked or looked down upon in most situations
- The raising of walls that we discussed should be comfortably taken down with trust.
- The need to be very defensive in otherwise non confrontational situations
- Snap decisions, impulse, and high reaction rates
- A fear of speaking true needs wants, and feelings in situations where they are required
- An overactive need to people-please
- High levels of harmful anxiety or even depression
- An inability to take responsibility for actions, personal needs, and feelings which can lead to self-neglect and poor health

- Dishonesty, either to oneself or one's partner
- High expectations of oneself or others, inflating the inability to reach one's goal of supposed perfection

## Find the Root of the Issue, and Separate the Person from the Problem

Many arguments seem one way on the surface but stem from a deeper-rooted issue below the surface. Have an open and honest dialogue with your partner and lay it all on the table so the two of you can sort through the issues and find the root of the cause. Furthermore, make sure to target the issue and not the person involved in the argument. The issue is the problem, not the person posing this issue. Do not attack your partner, but discuss the problem head-on to avoid any ambiguity or negative emotions. It is not, for instance, the person that you are truly frustrated with. It is the situation, so change it for your good and for the betterment of your partner. Your relationship will thank you, I'm sure.

The root of the matter is normally insecurity, an unsolved emotional issue, or something that one or the other person has been putting off for a while that is finally bubbling to the surface. Whatever the reason, try to make it your priority to pinpoint this main root so you can dig it up and hopefully resolve it first so the outlying issues will fall away with it. The smaller surface issues normally stem from the root cause of the problem as a whole.

For instance, if you are arguing with your partner about a fear that you have, let those walls down and confide in your partner. Let them know what scares you. It is not your partner that scares you, but it is the fear that you have projected upon that person. See how I separated that? Now, you can resolve it with honest dialogue.

Next, try to approach the issue as a team, not as two separate entities fighting. Fight the problem, not the person, and work as a team, together, to resolve it for the betterment of your relationship as a whole. Fight those fears off with encouragement, trust, and love and fall into each other's arms once it is resolved and tell each other how much you appreciate one another for having the strength to come forward and tackle such a difficult subject together.

## To Resolve, and Not to Attack

The intent of a healthy conflict resolution, and the approach thereof, is to calmly talk out the problem and find a compromise. Resolve the conflict and move on. The purpose of a disagreement is not to attack one another or point out who is wrong. It is to calmly explain each of your sides, find the root cause of the disagreement, and talk it all out.

Arguments are not supposed to be a tug-of-war. It is not about who wins or loses, but it is about the ability to resolve the issue proposed between the two of you. If you do win an argument, so to speak, there will still be residual resentment that will hurt the relationship and your partner, and it will lower your partner's self-esteem, which is not the goal that you want to achieve.

If all else fails, give your partner the benefit of the doubt and agree to disagree. If it is something that does not affect your health, your life, or your relationship, it is ok to just let it go, agree to disagree, and forget about it. This is for small matters that will not matter in the long run of your relationship. This is not a fix for big issues that directly affect one or both of you, but it is ok to just let some small things slide off your back and agree to disagree. It will minimize the need for further conflicts and it will diffuse the situation.

## Above All Else, Do Not Hold a Grudge

The detriment of relationships is holding a grudge. Getting negative feelings and pushing them down and away, only to have them pop up aggressively at inopportune moments is very damaging to a relationship. Always try to resolve an issue before this happens, and learn to forgive and trust your partner. Forgiveness is not only for the other person, but it is also beneficial to your wellbeing, peace of mind, and happiness. Forgiveness, when warranted, is a very healthy attribute of a good relationship that has a solid flow of communication.

Try not to stockpile your resentments over time. If something is bothering you, say it. If there is a conflict, resolve it. If the issue has been resolved, forgive it and let it slide off your back and into oblivion, but you must work things out as they come up, or they could turn into grudges and resentment. Communicate what is bothering you or your partner will not know what they did wrong to harbor that resentment, and it can make your partner resent you back. This is not healthy, so try to avoid it at all costs.

Forgiveness goes hand in hand with trust and respect. If you truly care for your partner, and your own wellbeing, learn to forgive them when they have done wrong, especially if they have apologized. Once the issue has been resolved, it is finished, and there is no need to bring it up again or use it as ammunition against your partner. This is petty, damaging, and wrong. It will not lead to a healthy relationship or communication therein.

# CHAPTER 3
## *Avoid Common Mistakes*

Mistakes will undoubtedly be made in any relationship. It's common, it's natural, and it's likely unavoidable. However, how we tackle those mistakes and react to them can make or break a relationship before it has the chance to blossom. Relationship communication mistakes can at times become sneaky and pop up when you least expect it, such as when you start finally getting comfortable enough with your partner to show your true colors. Communication is key here, and we will go over some of the most common mistakes that we must avoid and remedy with proper communication practices. Don't let a pattern of unhealthy communication practices form before you have the opportunity to identify and stem them. This chapter will help you get on the right track! Let's get started!

## Jumping to Conclusions/Assumptions

Rash decisions almost always have negative outcomes. Instead of prematurely assuming things about your partner without proper evidence, simply ask your partner so that your partner can clear the air, and no feelings are hurt. Be honest and come forth with any issues so that your partner can either confirm or deny them before an argument ensues. Assumptions can severely damage a relationship, so try to curb them before they break out and strike at your relationship.

This is a paraphrase from an ancient proverb, but it is very wise. The proverb says that it is not smart to answer a question that you yourself pose before hearing the correct answer from the person whom you are questioning. In order to get to the root of any situation, you must have adequate information and view the problem from all possible perspectives so that you get the context correct. Many things, when viewed out of context, can be severely misconstrued. When push comes to shove, listen with your ears, and do not assume with your eyes or your mind.

Oftentimes, we project our hang-ups from past relationships and past occurrences onto our current relationships. This is damaging for many reasons, but it will primarily damage your partner's trust of you and your ability to comfortably navigate the relationship without walking on eggshells. If your partner believes that you will always jump to conclusions, it can cause that person to pull back and withhold affection, emotions, thoughts, and intimacy from you. Your partner will try to tiptoe around situations, which will likely cause your assumptions to flare even more. Eliminate this realm of possibility by simply being open and honest with your partner and believing that they will do the same for you.

18

When you have an inkling about something before you do anything stop and breathe. Do not open your mouth or take any action until you give yourself ample time to process the information and assess the potential outcomes. Never accuse, and always ask. This will eliminate the feeling your partner could have upon being attacked without probable cause. Think about it this way: Would you want your partner to jump to conclusions before you have been given the opportunity to defend yourself or explain the situation?

If the answer is no, then do not do that to your partner. Even if your answer is yes, don't do it to your partner. Treat your partner with the respect that you would want to be given in that type of situation. Pause, give your partner the benefit of the doubt, allow your partner to have the room to speak and allow yourself to be open enough to dig deeper into the situation to find the truth behind where your assumptions lead you. This will help you cultivate a safer, more trusting, and healthy relationship that you and your partner can find comfort and not conflict in. Suspend your judgment and allow solid evidence and fulfilling conversations to take hold, and you will do just fine.

## Speaking on Impulse

Always think things through, and try not to blurt things out as soon as they pop into your head. Don't be one who word-vomits then picks up the pieces later. Try to hold your tongue and find the best routes for communication before you speak. This will save you a lot of headaches and conflicts down the road. Just because something comes to you, you have a piece that you think needs to be spoken, or you assume something, don't blurt it out without really thinking it through.

This also has a lot to do with timing. Bringing up issues, or starting an argument, at the wrong time or place can put a strain on your relationship. It is poor room-reading and communication to act on impulse and bring things up out of the blue or during inopportune times of the day.

Impulsivity can cause confusion and hurt, especially if it comes out of the blue and surprises your partner, who unfortunately cannot read your mind. Impulsivity can also trigger you to say things you may not mean or that may need to stay in your head to protect your partner from getting hurt, regardless of if that impulsive thought is true or not. In the end, it will only push your partner away and cause your partner to view you with potential anxiety as they are not sure what you will say next or when.

Don't allow your relationship to spiral out of control just because you cannot control your thoughts and your speech. Sometimes, too much communication and bluntness can be damaging. It's all about a balance and getting a good sense of your partner's sensitivities. Something can sound really good in your head but actually appear very hurtful from your partner's perspective.

# Raising Your Voice

This was touched on in the previous chapter but is important to note again because it is a common error that many make during the course of a relationship. Try not to have a short fuse and resort to yelling just to have your voice heard during angered or passionate moments where you converse. Having a loud voice actually does the opposite, as it creates tension and makes it harder to understand where you are coming from. Raised voices lead people to believe that you are speaking out of an irrational mindset and that your words stem from raw emotion and not calculated intellect.

# Sacrificing Your Own Happiness

Sacrificing your own happiness will wreak havoc on your emotional stability, mental health, and overall view of the world. It is not healthy for you, your partner, or your relationship and must be remedied in order to build a stable romantic foundation. Let's go over some of the ways we sacrifice our happiness and what we can do to change those actions for the better.

### Apologizing After Every Debacle

Apologizing, though you don't have to, after every situation where you assume you are in the wrong, is an unhealthy practice. It does not allow your partner to admit their wrongdoings, and it can severely damage the overall trust and stability of your relationship. It will create issues with your boundaries, cause an unhealthy pattern of negative consistency, and give your partner free rein to do whatever they want, as you will simply apologize for them. This is not fair to you or the relationship.

Apologizing too much also hurts your self-esteem. It causes confusion as you start questioning every action you make and feeling that you are not good enough to do anything right. It is a big factor in relationship anxiety and can mar the communication flow in a relationship. It can also cause a gut or impulse reaction where you start apologizing for every mistake in your relationship and your life. Tell yourself this: If you are apologizing for every aspect of your relationship, is the relationship worth sustaining? Why keep something that you always have to feel sorry for? Change your ways quickly, or you may slip into the mindset that you should get out lest your apologies overrule your life.

The best thing to do is, to be honest, and communicate openly with your partner. See things from both perspectives, and yes, apologize for what you do wrong, but do not excuse the wrongdoings of your partner. Furthermore, never apologize out of fear or to simply get your partner off your back. That is incredibly damaging, and it also enables negative behavior that will send you both spiraling out of control. There is no stability in this practice, so you will never find common ground or feel secure and safe in your relationship.

This simply communicates to your partner that they can do no wrong and that they can walk all over you with no consequence. Hold your partner accountable for your actions, and do not allow yourself to become a doormat. Do not allow dishonesty and deceit to seep into your relationship.

A great way to start combating this is to focus on your own inner strength and insecurities. By mending your own potentially broken spirit and self-consciousness, you can grow stronger in your relationship and stand on even ground.

## Being too Submissive

Don't roll over and expose your belly like a lamb for the slaughter, or it will damage your emotional, mental, and potentially physical wellbeing. Set up clear and concise boundaries at the start of the relationship and be consistent about it. Be caring, but firm, and reaffirm those boundaries without wavering so that there are stable ground and common understanding throughout your relationship. This will ultimately eliminate confusion in the long run.

Bending so far until you ultimately break and damage yourself is not a sign of undying love for your partner, it is a sign that you are harming your own wellbeing and the wellbeing of the relationship dynamic. In some ways, it is just as disrespectful to your partner as it is to yourself. You are not allowing your partner the room to grow as a person and contribute as much as they need to in the relationship.

Don't let your partner walk all over you. Set up boundaries, and stick to them so that you can strengthen yourself, strengthen your relationship, and keep yourself from being harmed.

## Being too Dependent On/Being a Crutch

It is nice to feel like you are needed, but there is a limit. If your partner becomes too dependent on you, it can become a burden for you and a handicap for your partner. It is actually detrimental to their wellbeing as a person to become too codependent because it makes it harder for them to stand on their own if the time ever came for that to happen. No matter how much you care for a person, you have to be practical and realistic and set up boundaries to preserve your own independence.

Set realistic goals and expectations for both you and your partner so that you can reach them as a team while strengthening and supporting the person who is being too dependent. Once that person reaches a sufficient level of strength, branch your goals just enough so that the dependent person can grow to meet their own needs and gain independence and

21

self-confidence. It does not have to happen all at once, but it must be consistent, and there must be progress for you both to be able to grow and for the relationship to survive.

If you take a tree, the relationship in this metaphor, and overburden one side while leaving the other side lacking in growth, the tree will bend over and eventually snap. Don't let the burdens your partner tosses at you bend the tree of your relationship. Share the burdens, overcome them together, and work on a team so that your relationship can grow to new heights and remain strong and firm.

Furthermore, resist the urge to fix every issue that comes up. Allow your partner to learn how to fix their own problems and pick themselves up after a fall. If you catch your partner every time they mess up or fail, they will learn that you will clean up their messes. If you let them self-correct, it will place less burden on you and allow your partner to grow as a person and become an equal, strengthening partner in the relationship.

The bottom line: Be each other's support systems while working as an equal team.

# Being Too Distant

Being too distant can be just as bad as being an emotional crutch. It's just the other side of the negative communication spectrum. If you are too silent, ignore issues, use passive aggression, suppress your emotions, give off an aura of resentment, and hold grudges, it can spell the downfall of your relationship and lead to deep-rooted hurt and chaos in a relationship. All of those suppressed emotions are going to bubble to the surface eventually, and when it ruptures, it will greatly damage the entire relationship and the parties involved. Why don't we go over how to fix some of these issues before they begin?

### The Silent Treatment

The silent treatment is, basically, the same as holding up a sign that says: "Back off! I don't want to let you in." This is bad. This makes your partner feel unappreciated and blocks off any attempts for your partner to try to remedy the situation for fear of making you more upset. It stops all possibilities of making things any better than they currently are. Negative emotions will continue to stew and get worse, neither of you will feel any relief, and the issue will never be resolved.

In any relationship, it is always best to have your issues out in the open, without aggression, and to be open enough and trusting enough to allow your partner in so that they can help fix the situation. It is unfair to be blatantly mad at someone without taking any action to make it better.

The silent treatment is just another way of phrasing passive-aggression. Sneering from the sidelines, making pointed snide comments, glaring from across the room, and blatantly removing yourself from the vicinity of your partner are examples of this. It is hurtful, it is unkind, and it will not make either of you feel better. Set your aggression aside and talk out your feelings. You will find that if you do this, you will easily makeup and embrace each other, and each other's differences, much easier.

### Pushing Down Your Emotions

Pushing your emotions down and never touching them or acknowledging that they are there will break you from the inside out. It is like putting a lid on a pressure cooker and letting the steam accumulate until the entire cooker cracks open, and the contents spill out in the worst possible way. It is best to get your emotions out in the open in a way that you can control before they have the opportunity to lash out and cause unnecessary pain.

# Commanding Actions

Commanding your partner is a way of belittling and looking down upon that person. It is destructive and it can lower the self-esteem of you both. If you are too abrasive and commanding in your communicative abilities, neither of you will truly feel at peace, nor will you be able to trust one another. It is about balance and a bit of give-and-take. Your relationship should be fluid and ever-changing for the positive. It should not be abrupt and full of orders and superfluous rules. It should be freeing, warm, comfortable, and stable. These next sections will go over some of the dos and don'ts you may want to take into account if you are in a position where you feel like you must command your partner.

### Ultimatums

Ultimatums are a defense mechanism that can harm your situation far more than it will help. Yes, they are direct, but it backs your partner into a wall that is hard to get out of. It leads to rash decisions, hurt, and betrayal. They will make your partner feel trapped, and it will put unnecessary pressure on your relationship. They are ingenuine and push away the root of the problem that has caused you to make such a rash decision. It is best to avoid them at all costs.

Instead of giving two choices that are unshakeable, compromise. Negotiate and discuss your issues in a way that gives your partner wiggle room to improve and make conscious decisions. Don't make up their mind for them. Chances are if you give only two choices, your partner will choose the one you don't really want. Don't get dominant and aggressive if you truly care about your partner. Make a way for you both to be happy without jeopardizing your entire relationship because you feel entitled to it.

## Nagging

Try not to harp on the little things, and once an issue has been discussed, don't bring it up over and over again. Let your partner self-correct, negotiate, and take time to process what needs to be done. This can lead to a massive amount of annoyance and frustration. Nobody likes to feel like their partner is their mom, following behind them at every turn with a broomstick and shouting commands.

Furthermore, don't bring up events from your partner's past that are long over and resolved. This can cause tension and stem your partner's trust for you, as your partner may think that you will simply judge them or jump to conclusions.

## Negotiate and Compromise

Again, compromise is key here. Before resulting in a command and conquer tactic that will lead to a negative dominant-submissive dynamic instead of a team effort, try to speak openly with your partner and become willing to hear their point of view. Put each of your opinions out in the open so you can see both perspectives and find common ground. This will eliminate the frustration and confusion of over-pleasing each other at the cost of your own happiness.

## Manipulation Leads to Destruction

We have gone over being over-dominant and over-submissive in a relationship, but within that realm of understanding, I will go over some of the reasons that manipulation in any of the forms discussed can be harmful. Examples of what manipulation lead to include:

- Self-esteem issues
- Codependency
- Resentment
- Lashing out
- Arguments
- A lack of trust
- Instability
- And more harmful outcomes

# Thinking Your Partner Can Read Your Mind

When you have a thought, pet peeve, pesky emotional issue, or anything that you want or need your partner to know but are afraid to ask, don't bite your tongue or let it sit and stew. Your partner cannot read your mind, and it is unfair of you to assume so or to get angry if they act in a way that is not consistent with your mindset. You must vocalize your issues, hang-ups, and emotions in order for you and your partner to bring them out into the open and resolve them as a team.

Understanding comes from proper communication. Tell your partner how you are feeling and be as open and honest as you can be. Try not to fear how they will act or feel because if they are truly invested in the relationship, they will listen regardless and try to find a compromise that is best for the both of you. Be truly honest, for honesty plays a big, big part here. If you are not honest, and your partner trusts you, they will not think to assume the real answer when you give them a false answer. This can lead to confusion, miscommunication, heartbreak, hypocrisy, and massive arguments and resentments down the road. There is no way to be a team and remain on the same page if you are not completely honest. Even small lies add up and poke holes in a relationship. Tread these waters carefully.

Do not assume that your partner knows you well enough to pick up on things, even if you give off body signals or otherwise. Reinforce your body signals with words. Cut out any possibility of ambiguity or jumping to conclusions. It will save you a lot of headaches in the long run, and it will help your partner trust you more.

Ask for what you need in the relationship and lay it all out on the table, lest you hit a massive roadblock in your relationship that will simply drive a wedge that could have been resolved easily in the beginning. Communicating in a healthy manner will eliminate the root causes of misunderstandings and future arguments, and it will be beneficial for you both if there are no guessing games, assumptions, and conclusion jumping. Just use your communication skills and talk it out!

## A Lack of Listening

An inability to listen, or simply choosing not to listen, is as bad as choosing not to speak up. It is a blatant form of disrespect for your partner, and it shows that you would rather ignore that person than hear their thoughts. Conflicts will never get resolved this way, and it can mean the detriment of your relationship in the long run. Be open enough to allow your partner to view you as a confidant so you can build upon your relationship and grow into a comforting solace of understanding, forgiveness, and dialogue.

## A Lack of Forgiveness and Acceptance

Look, everyone has their issues and things they need to work on. Every bit of progress made toward a better goal should be encouraged and built upon. Accept each other's differences, forgive when forgiveness is due, and learn to accept little things that you may not like but are ingrained in the person you chose to be with. You cannot change or fix a person.

Accept the things you cannot change and work together as a team to fix the things that can be changed. Use the tools learned thus far to talk through your issues together so that you can come to a better understanding as a couple and learn how to trust and forgive one another.

# CHAPTER 4
## How To Embrace Empathy

Empathy may seem like it is simply soft and sweet on the surface, all sugar plums and hugs and fairies, but it is a very powerful component of a healthy relationship. It is not all about sensitivity and butterflies but is a sensitive and gentle relationship attribute that is very important. It is a strong, constructive force of understanding, and it will help you *relate* to your partner, which is a key aspect here, and part of the nomenclature of a relationship. It is the relations between two individuals that create a relationship, after all. Therefore, being able to relate to your partner in a *relation*ship is a central component to note. Empathy is present at the very core of a true relationship.

## What is Empathy?

Since we're going to be covering empathy in this entire chapter, it is a good idea to clarify what empathy is, by definition, and how it applies to your relationship. Empathy is one's ability to connect with their partner's emotions and share those feelings with one another. It is also a compassionate, instinctive, and thoughtful ability to understand another person's feelings. It means to feel things alongside somebody else in order to gain a better understanding of those feelings and navigate them together compassionately. In this way, you can put yourself into the shoes of another and think as if those emotions are yours so you can gain the best consideration of them.

Empathy applies to a relationship in many ways. Empathy, within the scope of a relationship, boils down to how much you care about the wellbeing of your partner and their emotions to the same extent that you care about your own wellbeing and emotions. It's bringing your partner's emotions close and down to the level of your own. Proper empathy can make a huge difference in the health of your relationship.

There are actually three core forms of empathy, which I will go over next.

### Cognitive Empathy

Cognitive empathy is the conscious decision to view things from the perspective of another individual. It is what people refer to when they use the phrase "putting yourself into someone else's shoes." It is not the general definition of empathy on its own, but a branch of empathy itself that is very useful in a relationship for the benefit of both parties involved. It is a good technique for negotiations and compromises so you and your partner can find common ground.

Because this form of empathy is more conscious, it is easy to avoid getting wrapped up in the emotions of the situation, which is good in some cases. You don't have to engage the emotions, only understand them and view the perspective of another individual to gain insight. This is, arguably, the least emotive form of empathy. It is more practical, rational, and logical. It has to do with empathetic thought and not emotion.

## Emotional Empathy

This form of empathy, as its name suggests, is incredibly emotive. This is an endearing form of empathy that is wonderful to possess, but this is the one you need to be careful not to get too incredibly wrapped up in. With this form of empathy, you more directly feel the emotions of another person.

Think of a time where you have been watching a movie, and you cried during a sad part though you were in no way a part of the situation in the movie. This is a prime example of emotional empathy. Another example is feeling drawn to go adopt a new pet from the shelter after seeing a video of sad, abandoned animals. It is very easy to be swayed with this form of empathy, and while it is very sweet to be that way, tread carefully and keep it at a moderately high but healthy level.

It is good in that it helps us understand and connect with the feelings of our partners so that we know how to help them. It is a good skill for caretakers, mothers, healthcare workers, teachers, and those in a romantic relationship. It is a good tool to have when we need to respond to those in distress. Just try not to become a pushover or become manipulated by those who know you have a high level of compassion.

This form of empathy is what most think of when they hear the word empathy. It is deeply emotional, very kind, and very strong. It has often been referred to as emotional contagion, as you basically catch the emotions of others as if catching a cold from them. Just take your proverbial medicine, self-control, and you should be fine. Just don't go the complete opposite and become stoic and hardened.

## Compassionate Empathy

Compassionate empathy is another form of empathy that most think of when they hear the word empathy if they do not immediately think of the emotional empathy that we possess. In fact, emotional and compassionate empathy normally go hand in hand, but they have their differences.

Compassionate empathy is a lot like sympathy, but deeper. While sympathy is feeling emotions that are similar to your own, compassionate empathy is taking the feelings of others and understanding them while feeling concern or, well, compassion for those people. Compassionate empathy is also different from sympathy in that an individual with compassionate empathy is more likely to act upon those feelings and aid or lessen the problems posed by the affected people and their emotions. Compassionate empathy is less volatile and manipulatable than emotional empathy because the focus is not on your emotional tie to another individual, but the drive to help that individual. It is the most appropriate type of empathy for matters that are more vulnerable. It is a good middle ground between cognitive and emotional empathy. You won't become a basket case of emotions upon feeling what others feel, as with emotional empathy, and you won't be overly calculative with your understanding like cognitive empathy. You will calculate the situation, assess the feelings, but act upon them in a compassionate way that points the focus on the one you are helping without too intimately tying your emotions to theirs. You can be understanding and caring and give the best amount of help that you can in this situation.

### The Balance of the Three Empathies

Think of it like this. Emotional empathy is very emotional and affects you, cognitive empathy is less emotional and specifically targets the problem, and compassionate empathy creates a good balance by being right in the middle of the two, feeling emotive enough to want to help while focusing on the issue *and* the person involved. Make sure to properly balance these to remain stable in your use of empathy and learn to identify which form is best for certain situations. Apply reason, remain in control, open your heart, and use it to the betterment of yourself and your relationship.

# Empathy and Trust

Empathy is a big factor in the foundation of trust in a relationship, and it will deepen the intimacy and the feeling of connectivity in your relationship. You will feel more bonded, in a healthy way, and gain a sense of belonging with your partner. Empathy also makes it easier to notice when a problem occurs before it becomes a large issue because once you notice your partner's telling signals, which we will go into further in a moment, you can ask your partner openly about your perception of the signals they are giving off.

Their honesty, and your compassion, will help you both form a concrete solution to the potential issues hiding just below the surface of your partner's emotions. Being closely bonded and open enough in your relationship will help you utilize your empathy to reach below the surface and surmise how to help your partner.

Something that goes hand in hand with trust is forgiveness. When you become more empathetic and caring to your partner, your partner will feel listened to and appreciated. It will also make it easier to forgive one another once you gain the ability, through empathy, to catch a quicker and easier glimpse into your partner's point of view. You will be able to quickly react and avoid turning a blind eye to the negative emotions of your partner if the foundation of trust is there and forgiveness allows your heart to not cloud your eyes to these situations. It will ultimately strengthen your bond and bring you closer together.

The trust built with empathy can also help you foster teamwork in your relationship. This will allow you both to work together as a team toward common relationship goals, long-term life goals, and more.

## Don't Let Empathy Suck You Down a Dangerous Track

Empathy is good, and empathy is important, but don't let it overrule your other emotions so much that it drags you into the emotions of your partner in a negative way. Empathy is often misconstrued as feeling another's emotions at such a deep level that it influences your own emotions. This is not correct, and it is a dangerous view to have.

Empathy is very different from the occurrence of you feeding off the emotions of your partner. This occurs when your emotional empathy gets out of control. This is a very dangerous situation that can lead to codependency. It can make it very hard, also, to support your partner if you are drowning in their emotional influence. If you get roped into their complicated web of emotions, you will not be able to sort through your feelings, let along with theirs. Rather, try to help your partner unravel their web while maintaining a firm and steady, but compassionate, ground. This is where cognitive empathy comes into play. Keep your self-identity intact and use your resolve to help them wade through the waters of whatever they are going through.

Don't get caught up in your own emotions, separate from but influenced mildly by your perception of your partner's, in the process, however. Process your emotions, yes, but try not to confuse them with your partner's specific emotions. If you do, the situation could get misconstrued, and you could jump to conclusions and assumptions and cause a miscommunication that could make the situation worse.

Be attentive. Don't be an emotional crutch, so to speak, but be attentive and support your partner. Attentively and genuinely give your partner the attention that they deserve in a healthy manner, without letting your attention spiral into an alteration of your own mood.

## Use Empathic Listening to Validate Your Partner

Empathy helps to validate the emotions of your partner. In order to validate your partner, you need to listen to them. Don't just hear them speak, but actively and attentively listen. Give your partner your full attention, and then if they want you to reply, you can, with compassion and potential advice. Listening sincerely and intently, without interrupting your partner, is a huge sign of respect, and it shows genuine appreciation for your partner as a person.

Listening also helps you truly understand where your partner is coming from, making it much easier to empathize with them. Listen beyond the words and feel the emotions behind those words and the body language your partner portrays. Empathic listening is very strengthening and healthy for your relationship, and it will build a firm foundation for you and your partner.

When following up with your empathic listening, make sure to pay attention to and remember important details from the conversations. Follow up a few hours, days, or weeks later, depending on the situation, so that your partner will know you truly listened. This lets them know that they communicated clearly and accurately to you, and it builds solid trust between the two of you.

Follow up empathic listening with phrases such as these to open the best communication pathways with your partner:

- "Last week you mentioned...and how are you feeling about it this week?"
- "I just wanted to check up with you about what you said to me the other day. Has anything changed?"
- "You seemed upset the other day. How are you feeling now, and can I help in any way?"
- "I remember you said...so is there anything I can do to make things easier for you today?"
- "You sound frustrated. What can I do to make things better for you?"

You can also use more advanced validation techniques, which offer to your partner signs that you understand their feelings more deeply than the fact that you simply listened. Asking how they feel and similar phrases are beneficial, but they are a bit simplistic on the surface. Here are some deeper phrases that show a more in-depth understanding of the emotions that your partner may be feeling:

- "That looks like it took a lot of work and dedication! I am so proud of you, and I'm sure you must feel great for doing such an amazing job!"
- "You have every right to feel the way that you do. I know that I would go insane if I had to deal with a situation like that! You are handling it much better than I would, and that is so great! I'm here for you, and I support how you are handling this."
- "It is completely healthy to feel that way. The hurt you feel is how anyone would feel in that situation, and I am so sorry that this has happened to you."
- "I am so sorry for confusing you the other day. You are right to feel frustrated. I apologize for not understanding your point of view at the time."
- "I understand that you are scared. It would be hard not to be in that position. Is there anything I can do to make you feel safer and to lift your spirits?"

31

See? This is a lot more in-depth than a phrase such as "I understand that you are anxious about this." It gives an extra layer of understanding. "I understand that you are anxious about this, because I would be too. Being yelled at or belittled is unfair to you, and you have every right to feel upset," is a much more in-depth version of the first phrase. If you are sure that your partner is feeling a certain way, after thoroughly listening to them, then this dialogue, rich in a deeper understanding of the situation, may be a good idea. The identification of the specific emotion, instead of a blanket phrase such as "I'm sorry you are upset," is a great way to reveal that you can pick up on your partner's emotions accurately.

## Body Language and Signals

Be mindful of those bodily communication signals we talked about in the first few chapters. Pick up on those signals as best as you can and assess the emotional situation of your partner. Step into their shoes to an extent and find their perspective. That way, you can help them to the best of your ability, and you can come down to their level to meet them eye-to-eye.

Take care to ensure that you do not use this opportunity to look down upon your partner from a higher standing, for this can make your partner feel inferior. It will have a negative effect. Don't use your strength in this position, during a very vulnerable situation for your partner, to get any kind of upper hand or superiority complex. Do not lord over your partner the fact that in this particular situation, you are more emotionally stable. Rather, pick up on their emotions through the use of compassion and empathy and help your partner the best way you can. Empathize with them by being kind and genuine in asking questions, showing your concern, and letting your partner know that you are there for them.

Signals in this situation include things like slumped shoulders, frowns, averted eyes, and crossed arms. Pick up on these signals to determine the next best step, and do not be abrasive or it will just throw them deeper into their negative body language and emotions. Try to get to know your partner well enough through dialogue and compassionate questions so that you will know the signs that they give off. That way, when you see these signs, you can assist and give aid to your partner.

Use your strength in these situations to share it with your partner through support, and give off signals of compassion and not superiority. Give a gentle smile, be open in your body language, and be someone that your partner can fall back on and embrace. Open your eyes and your arms to them, and exude positive emotions and encouragement so that they feel safe and secure in your arms. This will build trust and intimacy. It ties very close, in fact, to what we have talked about thus far regarding trust and respect. If you respect your partner, it will show through the kindness you share in these situations. They will respect you more for it, and trust you in hard situations.

## Don't Try to Fix Every Issue

For the truly empathetic, this can be a tough one. When you hear your partner out and feel that they are hurting, it is common to want to try to fix every issue. This can be good, at times, but in many cases your partner needs to be able to sort things out on their own. This helps them build personal strength and character. The best thing you can do is be there for them. Be a shoulder to cry on and an ear to listen. Many people need to open the flood gates and let everything out in order to piece it all together. You don't have to respond in this case, simply listen.

When somebody is deeply distraught, or there are many emotions going on in their head, it is hard to make sense of it. In the turmoil of emotion, many things seem to be spinning into chaos on the inside. When somebody has the opportunity to voice their emotions, it becomes a more tangible thing that can be pieced together. It's easier for people to voice these emotions if there is someone who will listen. That is why many people pay money to a therapist in order to voice their feelings. You can be the stand-in for your partner and allow them the outlet they need to bounce off ideas and emotions. Once they do, it will be easier for them to make sense of the storm inside.

If they speak and ask for advice, you may offer it. Just don't try to jump right in there and offer advice until your partner is ready. They need time to process every side of the issue, and that's ok.

Saying invalidating phrases, however well-intentioned they may be, is a very bad idea. In fact, it is just about the worst thing you can do in a particularly sensitive or negative emotional situation. Here is a list of phrases you should absolutely avoid in these situations, for your and your partner's own wellbeing:

- "That's not true!"
- "This is what you need to do..."
- "Don't worry about it."
- "Hey, it could be worse!"
- "Let it go."
- "Just ignore it!"
- "Someday, it will get better."
- "I feel you, one time this happened to me..."
- A funny joke or sarcastic remark to deflect their emotions

Saying phrases such as the ones above trivializes the emotions of your partner, and that is not what you should do. It is the opposite of empathetic to try to coerce your partner to ignore, push down, or laugh off their emotions. As I said before, your partner needs to feel and work through their emotions. Processing your emotions is emotionally healthy, and it helps you learn from it and overcome it. If you ignore it or push it away, it will never get resolved. Furthermore, turning their problems into a joke makes them feel disrespected and gives off the impression that you were never truly listening in the first place. Tread carefully here, and when in doubt, stay silent and simply listen.

# CHAPTER 5
## *Create Deeper Intimacy*

As to not beat around the proverbial bush, we all know that intimacy is closely intertwined with most romantic relationships, and to put it bluntly, people like to have sex. When you tie sexual intimacy into a romantic and steady relationship, however, a deeper level of communication must occur in order for you both to get the most out of the encounter. It will also cultivate the benefit of fostering a closer relationship overall.

Better than sex alone, in your relationship, is the ability to have fulfilling sexual encounters that make you both feel appreciated, closely bonded, and satisfied. The key to this is proper communication in the bedroom. In order for this to occur, you have to both feel that your voice has been heard so that you are both comfortable and feel the best from each sexual encounter. Sex isn't all about the body after all, it's about the experience, and it has a lot to do with the words you both say.

That isn't to say that you don't use your body and non-vocal communication during sex, however. You also have to understand the more subtle forms of sexual communication that go beyond words, such as body language, physical touch, and wordless sounds. We will go into that further in a moment.

Sex involves a lot of give-and-take. It also involves consent, voicing your sexual needs, wants, and aversions, and compromising so that neither you nor your partner feels unsatisfied or frustrated. This all involves proper communication in order to set up boundaries, sexual preferences, and more. You both want your needs to be met, and the best way to accomplish this is to voice your needs and wants openly with your partner and to listen when they voice theirs.

Furthermore, communication outside the bedroom is key to a good sex life within the bedroom. Your partner is much more likely to jump in bed with you if they feel appreciated, validated, listened to, and safe. Trust is a key factor here as well. The ability to trust your partner outside the bedroom will make it so much easier to feel comfortable inside the bedroom. We will go over how communication out of the bedroom transitions into the bedroom in this chapter as well.

Let's go over some ways to get the most out of your sexual communication and cultivate a healthy basis for your sexual encounters in your relationship through communication.

## Set Proper Boundaries and Expectations

Consent is key, and it must be given in any and all sexual situations. Once you set up the consensual agreements, start talking about your needs and your wants, comforts, and discomforts, and encourage your partner to do the same so you can have a common ground and a basis for compromise if the situation warrants it. Plus, if you don't get everything out in the open right off the bat when it comes to your mind you will forget it and be sexually displeased. You will also hold off from saying it so long that you will push it down and it will distract you during sex as you are constantly thinking about how much you wish you had voiced it beforehand. It's always better to say what is on your mind regarding sex than to keep it in and cause embarrassment or regret after the fact.

Setting up proper boundaries for sex is a way to protect both yourself and your partner, which is important if you honestly care about yourself and about your partner. Make it clear before you get serious in the relationship about what makes you uncomfortable, what you are ok with, and what is negotiable once you have had time to get comfortable with your partner. Never jump into any sexual encounter, regardless of the length of your relationship, without first setting up these boundaries to protect yourself, your partner, and your relationship. For instance, if you are comfortable kissing, having consensual missionary sex, and participating in foreplay, but are not comfortable with things such as anal sex, bondage, and more adventurous sexual kinks, make that well known before you strip and get down to business. It will save you a lot of embarrassment, discomfort, and frustration in the long run.

In order to be comfortable in your relationship, and to avoid conflict and distress, proper boundaries and expectations for sexual encounters must be discussed. There needs to be a clearly defined divide between what is ok and what crosses a line. Make sure you discuss what makes you uncomfortable and make sure you listen to what makes your partner uncomfortable in order to avoid any negative situations. Also, make sure that you are firm in your decisions if your partner does ever cross a line, that way, confusion will not spiral out of control, and your partner won't get the wrong idea. The best advice I can give you here is to be as honest as you can. Don't let the embarrassment of telling your partner you are not ok with something to overrule your own levels of comfort. It will only make it harder and more embarrassing further down the road.

Next, discuss what both you and your partner want out of the encounter. Voice what makes you feel good and what does not, and set up those guidelines so that you can have the most enjoyable time that you can while your partner feels the same. For example, tell your partner what areas of your body you are comfortable with them touching and which you are not comfortable with. You can also discuss positions you are comfortable with, whether or not certain kinks are ok, and what really gets you fired up.

Then, talk about specifics. What do you want to do during your next sexual encounter? Let your partner know what you are expecting, ask what they want to do, where they want to be touched, and more. Make it sexy, talk about what would curl your toes, where you want to be kissed, what positions would drive you wild, and more. It will make the sex enjoyable, keep your partner interested in what will turn you on, and it will allow you both to get fired up and going without floundering around or scrambling to get to the right spot. You can't read each other's minds, so read each other's lips.

If you talk about the positions you would like to use, where you want to be touched, what kinds of foreplay you would like to perform to get you both hot and bothered, and more, it can really spice up the sex, and it will also boost the sexual tension in the room as you talk through what you are going to do to one another. It will make the whole scenario more pleasurable for the both of you, and you'll both be able to strike while the iron is hot.

## Communicate During Intimacy

Now, we all know that the biggest and best part of sex is the physical sensations; however, communication is just as stimulating and just as important. While you are intimate with your partner, it is a good idea to constantly communicate what feels good, what doesn't, and what you are enjoying about your partner. Phrases such as "How does this feel?", "Is this comfortable?", and "Do you like this?" are good starting points.

Furthermore, communicate what you like about what is happening, as this makes your partner feel good and it boosts their confidence if they know that they are doing a good job. You can use verbal or nonverbal communication here, such as a smile, passionate kisses, phrases like "This feels so good", and more to foster this positive communication. Even certain noises give off good communication during a sexual encounter.

Lastly, compliments and sweet words are beneficial during sex. Even building up to it, you can comment on how beautiful, handsome, or sexy your partner is, which will give them confidence and drive once you intertwine. Passionate sex is fueled just as much by ardent words as it is by physical stimulation.

## Get Comfortable with the Words

A lot of the time, people avoid talking about sex before doing the act because certain words or phrases make them uncomfortable. This can lead to a bit of a roadblock while discussing and engaging in sexual intercourse because it makes it harder to talk through what is happening. If the words make you uncomfortable, try getting more familiar with them so you can be more comfortable during sex and while talking about it. Voice your discomfort with your partner and talk through this together.

You may even be able to find words to replace the ones that make you uncomfortable so that it will be easier to speak about them. You can try using euphemisms for certain phrases and body parts to minimize confusion and unease. For instance, you can say: "I would like for you to go inside me," instead of saying: "I want to be penetrated" or "I'd like to have vaginal intercourse." Another example could be that you are uncomfortable saying words such as penis, vagina, or anus. You can change these words to something less anatomical or blunt, such as changing penis to erection, member, shaft, or dick or some unique nickname you come up with.

Furthermore, if, after talking it through with your partner and attempting to get comfortable with it, you are still uncomfortable with certain words or phrases, you could use hand gestures or physical communication to get the point across. In the end, whatever makes you most comfortable is the best choice. Being comfortable and relaxed makes sex much more enjoyable for you both, and less awkward.

## Use that Body!

Do you remember how we talked about body language and physical communication? This seriously comes into play here with sexual intimacy. The ability for your partner to pick up on sexual and romantic cues will make transitioning into the bedroom, and into sex, a lot more fluid and enjoyable. It's all about giving off the right signals. Your body is its own communication tool, not just your lips and voice. Use your body language and physical touch to create a deep, intimate bond with your partner and feel your way through intimacy in the most sensual, connected way you can. Communicate with touch, feel your partner's body on yours, and use your eyes, lips, mouth, and whatever other parts of yourself that you can to show your partner how you feel! This can be really fun, and it is a very good tactic in the bedroom.

### Physical Touch

The most literal use of your body in a sexual encounter is your use of physical touch. Use the power of this sensual form of communication to your advantage and wow your partner while leading them down a path they can easily follow with the right physical cues. Pepper passionate kisses on your partner's body to show just how eager you are to appreciate their body. Kiss their neck to insinuate you are in the mood, get them fired up, and let them know you want the same treatment right back! You can even be direct and, with your partner's consent, place your hand on their erogenous zones or their hand on yours. Raise the temperature of your sexual passion by making it impossible for your partner to miss what your intentions are! Act like love-struck teens again and play footsies, wink at them, and plant a sultry kiss on your partner's lips. I'm sure your partner will get the message really quick! If they don't, there are other ways to get your partner's attention! More on that next.

38

## Body Language

Body language can either dampen the heat of romance or spice it up! Turning your body away from your partner, for instance, or lying in a closed-off position, can give off the vibe that you don't want to be touched. Biting your lip and staring your partner up and down, however, can give them the signal that you are ready for some kissing action. It's all in the subtle ways that you portray yourself to your partner. Something as simple as a smile, even, can make you seem open and inviting to your partner. Use your body to your advantage to give off the best signals to your partner, even if they are indirect. It will show you just how much your partner pays attention to you, and how closely bonded you are if you notice that they pick up on your innuendos.

Some common body language signs we show during intimacy, even if we don't realize it at the time, are as simple as closing your eyes during a pleasurable experience, arching your back during enjoyable intercourse, grasping the sheets uncontrollably to ground yourself as your world is shaken by the feeling of your partner's body on yours, and parting your lips slightly in ecstasy.

More bold or conscious forms of body language communication during intimacy are commonplace as well, and we are more aware of the fact that we do them. When you turn your head a certain way to expose your neck to your partner, for instance, it shows that you are letting your walls down and opening yourself up to your partner. It also indicates vulnerability and trust as you send off a signal that you want to be kissed all over your body and that you want them to come closer, possibly. Even the way you glance at your partner, wink, smile, and turn your body toward them shows undeniable invitations that you want them to come closer to you.

If all else fails, you can always be more direct in how you communicate your sexual desires. If you are in the mood for a hot and steamy interaction, you can always tease your partner by walking toward the bedroom and leaning against the doorframe in a provocative way. You can also unbutton your shirt, expose skin, and run your hands down your body while mimicking sexually pleasing movements. If that does not catch their eye, there is always the option of undressing and coyly showing off that body as you walk away. They will probably come after you like a dog after a bone!

## Sound

The right sounds can make your intimacy heat up faster than the next gasp that escapes your lips. Wordless noises can say as much, if not more, than any words you can speak to your partner. It is a primal form of communication that can turn on your partner, lead them to all the right places, and communicate just what you are feeling. For instance, an involuntary moan when your partner touches and kisses just the right spot can make a passionate moment turn into a symphony of pleasure. Making small noises when your partner kisses you in certain places can unlock a fervent part of their brain that can raise your intimacy to the next level. Show your partner how you feel and let your lips release all the signs they need to know that you are enjoying their actions. These sounds communicate emotions, intentions, sensations, and so much more. So, soundproof that room and make your own sensual music with your partner until the sun rises.

Use your natural sexual sounds to egg your partner on and create a more fervent bedroom environment. Give your partner positive feedback as they pleasure you so that without having to look up from what they are doing, they can hear your pleasure like music to their ears. Don't hold back your moans, sighs, heavy breathing, and your little squeaks of pleasure, because it is a natural way through which we communicate how much we enjoy the moment when our lips and brains are busy elsewhere. Just let it flow out as naturally as the sensations flowing over your skin, through your nerves, and in your core. If you do it often enough, and it turns your partner on, you may get to hear some happy noises from them as well!

## Try Not to Jump to Conclusions

Jumping to the wrong conclusions can cause your partner to jump right out of bed. Communicate during sex, and do not simply assume your partner's needs and wants. This is where consent comes in, as well as what you two have discussed about what you expect and what you would like or dislike in the bedroom. When in doubt, ask your partner! Sex is not a silent act, as many people know.

If you assume what your partner wants and just go for it without talking it through, you can leave them unsatisfied and come out feeling like a fool. When in doubt, always ask questions and communication throughout a sexual encounter. It is always better to ask than to assume. It doesn't have to be complicated, either. Simply ask: "Is this ok?" or "Does this feel good?", and your partner will be able to openly communicate what they need, want, and like. You can be content knowing that you have done everything that they have voiced wanting you to do, and that you have not crossed any lines. This can build trust and respect, and if they are happy, they will likely reciprocate and show you the same respect.

## Let Your Partner Know That You Appreciate Them

Compliments are a wonderful way to heat up the mood, and it makes sex more fluid and enjoyable when the self-confidences of the people involved are lifted. Sweet nothings, passionate talks outside and inside the bedroom, body language as you look your partner over, and more really shows your partner how much they mean to you and how affected you are by their presence.

Partners tend to appreciate each other's bodies more if they feel appreciated on the inside. An intimate relational bond between two partners is heavily influenced by how they feel for one another. Before you enter the bedroom, always resolve any conflicts you have and make sure your partner knows how you feel in a non-sexual way. This will uplift spirits, sex drives, and affection for one another in the long run.

Another way to appreciate your partner before and after sex is to do sweet things for them throughout the day. It will warm them up to you, make them feel appreciated, and communicate how much you care for them. It is not directly linked to sex, but it improves your relationship and may lead to them showing how much they appreciate *you* in bed if you know what I mean. Communicating in sweet ways to your partner is a great way to improve and strengthen your relationship, and it is really nice to show them a bit of love every once in a while, in a way that isn't sexual. It lets them know that sex is not the only thing on your mind, yet it will translate well into the bedroom as you both learn to love and support one another. You can also do sweet, appreciative things for your partner that can lead to the bedroom, such as a nice massage, a trail of flower petals to the bed, draw them a nice hot bath, pour them a glass of wine, light some candles for them, and more. This is a great way to make your partner feel cared for while enticing them to reciprocate in the bedroom.

## Be Open to New Things

Being adventurous and bouncing new and exciting ideas off one another in the bedroom is a great way to spice up the relationship and keep it alive. Spontaneity, within the realms of your agreed upon consensual boundaries, is very exciting and is its own stimulating form of intimate dialogue. As we discussed, communication is not only verbal. A bit of surprise and imagination through your physical touch communicates new and exciting areas of your intimate relationship that you may have never known were there.

Examples of new things you can try as a couple include:

- Sex positions (i.e., missionary, cowgirl, doggy-style, wheelbarrow,
- Toys (i.e., vibrators, butt plugs, etc.)
- Role-play (i.e., student and professor, little red riding hood and the big bad wolf, naughty wife and plumber, vampire and victim, etc.)
- Watching sexy movies or pornography together to get ideas
- Sexy talk/dirty talk

- Food play (i.e., ice cream, chocolate syrup, whipped cream, maple syrup, etc.)
- Temperature play (safely)
- Change power roles (i.e., dominant versus submissive)
- Foreplay techniques
- Tantric sex
- Light bondage (i.e., silk scarves, fuzzy handcuffs, etc.)
- Mutual masturbation
- Anal sex
- Turning the lights off or dimming them
- Playing sexy music
- Massage with soothing oils
- Move outside the bedroom (i.e., kitchen table, floor, couch, shower, etc.)
- Read the Kama Sutra
- Make a personal sex tape (Just don't distribute it!)
- And more!

## Ask, and You Shall Receive

Ask your partner for what you want out of the sexual encounter so they can please you without reading your mind. You can even do it in a sexy way by pleading with sultry whispers in your partner's ear, biting your lip and sliding your hands over your body where you want to be touched, and more. Drive your partner crazy so that there is no room for them to say no, and you can fall head over heels for each other in bed when the time comes.

## Communication as a Sexual Guidance Tool

Use communication to guide your partner through your sexual encounters. You can even role-play a bit here and act as your partner is brand new to all of this. If they are ok with it, you can role-play that your partner is still a virgin and that you are the teacher showing them the ropes. Whatever way you choose, guidance is imperative, and it can be very sexy. For your partner to know how to please you, and vice versa, you have to be able to communicate your specific needs and desires. Phrases that are associated with this during sex include: "more", "over here", "go down a bit", "faster", "slower", "harder", "softer", and more.

Guide and show your partner what you want and exactly how you want it. It can turn them on and make the situation fun as you guide each other through pleasurable moments. You can even take your partner's hand and move it to where you want to be touched. Use your own hand and do on them what you want to be done to yourself, or you can even touch yourself to tease them and get them eager to bat your hand to the side and go to town.

## Start Outside the Bedroom

The best way to get the most out of your intimate relationship is to start outside the bedroom. Build up to it. Tease and entice your partner with subtle touches, whispered sweet nothings, sneak peeks into what is to be expected once the time comes for you to intertwine, and discussions about what will make you both happy in the bedroom.

You can also start the sexual tension outside of the bedroom. Tease your partner by leaving a trail of clothing to the bedroom. Start with the shirt, the pants, the underwear, and at the end of the clothing rainbow will be you, in all of your glory! You can also leave little suggestive notes around the house, send naughty pictures and messages, and more! Gentle dirty talk throughout the day is a good tactic, too, but only if you think your partner will be ok with it. Building up the sexual tension throughout the day is a great way to get your partner ready to pounce when the time comes! Do just enough to give your partner a sneak peek and leave them begging for the main course.

Another important factor of out-of-bedroom communication that feeds into bedroom time is the establishment of trust and supportive communication. If throughout your relationship, in non-sexual situations, you have maintained relationship stability and respectful communication, that respect you hold for one another, the comfort you share in each other, and the attraction you will have built up will lead to a much more enjoyable encounter in intimate situations. If you have a rocky relationship full of arguments, distrust, and anger outside of the bedroom, it won't magically translate into a passionate and enjoyable sex life despite what some movies and books portray.

Make sure your communication separate from intimate communication is stable first before you build upon your intimacy. It will make you both feel more loved, more comfortable, and more compatible in the bedroom if you do.

# CHAPTER 6
## *Gain Healthy Conflict Resolution In Your Relationship And Mend Bridges*

As we discussed earlier in this book, conflict resolution is imperative for the stability of a relationship. Point-blank, if a relationship is rocky and full of resentment and anger, it will crumble and fall apart over time. Every time a conflict is not resolved, a hairline fracture sneaks into the foundation of your relationship, and the pressure of all of the suppressed emotions will cause that foundation to crack and break loose. In this chapter, I'm going to show you how to prevent this from happening and how to mend that foundation with proper communication techniques and advice.

We've gone over how to resolve any conflict, but how about preventing conflict from occurring? What about the aftermath of conflict? Well, now that we know how to resolve a conflict, let's figure out how to repair those broken pieces after the fact. We'll also come up with some good ways to prevent the conflict from even starting. Let's get started, shall we?

## How to Prevent Conflict

Conflict prevention is essential in a relationship, and it is just as essential as conflict resolution. When you stop a conflict from happening, in a healthy way, you won't have to fix the emotional trauma later on down the road. We're going to go over some concrete ways to help you prevent future conflicts and strengthen your communication with your partner.

### Don't Always Try to Be Right.

Getting in the last word may give you instant gratification. Feeling that you are always right and that you know everything may make you happy at the moment, but I promise you it won't make you happy in the long-run. Being arrogant enough to think that you can never be wrong is like taking the fast-track into a single-town. You will never be able to resolve anything, never be able to discuss anything with your partner, and never be able to grow as a couple.

Relationships are all about to give and take. Your partner has to be right sometimes, and you are going to be wrong sometimes. You have to learn to accept that if you want to have a healthy relationship. If you don't, it will only lower your self-esteem over time and severely harm your partner. If your partner feels like they are always wrong, it will make them feel bad, and it will also cause a lot of frustration. You can not be right all of the time, and that is ok. You have to accept that you may have faults, but that does not have to be a bad thing. You can work as a team with your partner and overcome those faults together. If you overcome them, you can grow and learn from your mistakes.

If you truly care for your partner, know that you don't have to be right all the time. The person you choose to be with is someone you should love, and if you really love them, you appreciate who they are and know that they are smart enough to understand what is going on most of the time. Don't degrade your partner and assume that they are never right, because if that is true, and your partner is never right, what is the point of being in that relationship in the first place? Understand that coming to a compromise, standing on common ground, and accepting defeat at times are much more positive and enlightening than being stubborn. Reach conclusions together as a team, and stand together to overcome issues in your relationship. Strengthen that bond, which is so important in a relationship, and it will make you feel so much happier. I guarantee it.

Look at it this way: Would you want your partner to patronize you? Belittle you? Make you feel like you are never right, and that you are not smart? I don't believe you would. Therefore, don't do the same to your partner, who you care about. Take a second and empathize. See the issue from their perspective, and try to realize where they are coming from. Neither of you can be right all the time, and I'm not saying you are wrong all of the time, but there is a balance that must be maintained. Just talk things out with your partner and try to fix things together, instead of making every discussion a battle, and you will both come out much happier and prevent arguments.

## Prevent Issues, but Don't Ignore Issues

We are talking about preventing heated, aggressive arguments in this chapter. We are not discussing how to avoid confrontation entirely. When there is an issue, it needs to be brought to light and handled with maturity, proper communication, and respect. Prevent the frustration and abrasion while discussing the root issue that is bothering you, and don't attack your partner. Work as a team, grow together, and never push things away out of fear or embarrassment, or they will never be resolved. Even little things build up over time, so it's best to nip them in the bud before that happens! Eliminate the possibility of misunderstandings and blown gaskets!

If you don't confront the issue, you will slowly boil inside and burst like a pressurized pot of water, harming your relationship with your partner in potentially irreversible ways. Take the time to think things through and present your thoughts to your partner without fear. If you truly trust your partner, there is no need to fear their reaction anyway! Communication is always better than silence, and your partner will trust and respect you more if you are open and honest with them. Take this as an opportunity to strengthen your bond and grow closer as a team while you tackle tough issues together!

45

## Choose Your Battles Wisely

If you nit-pick and harbor resentment after every little thing your partner does wrong, it will cause a problem. Your partner will grow distant and less likely to come to you with issues if they fear that you will only respond with anger and aggravation. Let the small things slide off your back, and try to confront the bigger things that truly affect your relationship so you can remain close and more than tolerate one another.

For example, an issue you should let roll off your back would be something like your partner deciding that they'd rather fold clothes than roll them up. Yeah, maybe it's annoying, but at the end of the day, the clothes still get put up. Don't nag your partner when they are just trying to help. It may not be exactly the way you would do it, but that's ok. They are still putting in the effort, which is what matters.

Now, if it's a big issue like your partner neglecting their promises or cheating on you, then yeah, you can express a fair amount of anger. No one would blame you for that, just resolve it in a mature way. The little things, however, are not going to matter a week from now, or a year, or ten years. Avoid inflicting lasting damage over something that is fleeting and unrelated to your relationship in the long-run. Choose your battles, be empathetic, and let yourself relax every once in a while. It will turn out ok, I promise.

## Don't Project Personal or Unrelated Problems onto Your Partner.

One of the most harmful things you can do is project negative emotions onto your partner or blame them for issues unrelated to them. This is not to say you can't confide in your partner, but I'm talking about those times when you are just so frustrated with the day that you snapped at your partner when they did nothing wrong. If you are upset and feel like you are about to snap, excuse yourself and walk away for a bit to calm down. Your partner is there for you. They will comfort you, support you, and love you, so don't push them away or hurt them just because you are hurt. Take responsibility for your own emotions and respect your partner's wellbeing by letting your anxieties and frustrations cool down before you let them loose on someone who only wants to help. If you don't, it will cause those fractures in your relationship that we discussed. If you turn your partner into an unnecessary enemy or a target for negative emotions, it will only lead to a negative outcome for your relationship. Embrace your partner, express your feelings, and let them in. Let your walls down, and that pent-up frustration will subside. Then, you can sort through the emotions that are struggling to escape and strike out at anyone within arm's reach.

Projection is a defense mechanism, but it doesn't have to be! Instead of diverting your emotions to your partner to lessen their effects on you, use your partner as support and let your walls down. Express your emotions, but don't lash out. This will make it impossible for your partner to help and support you because you will likely hurt them and make them get angry right back at you. Tell your partner how you are feeling, apologize if you do catch yourself projecting, and heal together.

Another good mechanism to use in order to avoid projection is to identify the cause of your feelings before you project them onto your partner. Also, take responsibility for your own insecurities and realize that your partner does not deserve to share the burden of your emotions. You don't want to wish negative emotions onto someone you care about, do you? Instead, let them help you, and work through it together so that you feel better and your partner does not get hurt in the crossfire.

**Don't Push Down Your Emotions.**

If you suppress your emotions, you either become numb to them or explode over time. This is not healthy for you or your relationship. Always communicate your emotions to your partner, or let them out in another healthy way, to prevent snapping at them and causing aggression. When you work together as a team to resolve an issue or find a healthy outlet to release the pressure of your emotions, you will become stronger as a person, stronger as a couple, and you will not grow to resent your partner over ill-expressed issues and misunderstandings.

When you suppress your feelings, it also can make your partner feel unimportant or unappreciated. They may feel that you have grown distant, and you do not trust them enough to open up to them and confide in their comfort and love. Your partner is there for you with open arms. They should be your rock, your support, and your confidence. If you can't let your walls down and express your emotions to them, it can make them feel unneeded and useless as a partner. When you are in a relationship, you become a team, and part of being a team involves helping one another and being honest. If you can be honest and expressive with your partner, you can build your trust and tackle anything together!

Furthermore, suppressing your emotions can build stress up in your mind, and it can cause negative outcomes for your body. When you stress, you release cortisol, which can wreak havoc on your energy levels, blood pressure, anxiety levels, heart rate, and more. When you start to feel bad, it can make it harder to control the emotions you are pushing down, creating pressure, and fracturing you mentally, emotionally, and physically. This will translate badly into your relationship, and you don't want that. Let your emotions out in a healthy way, so they don't cause problems in your relationship. Let them out in a calm way, and they will not escape from your grasp and cause damage in every area of your life, including your relationships.

If you have to, it is perfectly ok to let your emotions out on someone other than your partner, as long as you make sure they know that you are ok and that you are not avoiding them due to anger. There are a lot of ways to express and release emotions in a healthy way, and none of these ways are wrong! Anything you can do to calm down is ok, and your way may be different than your partner's. That is ok! Your outlets for emotional release may even be different than my examples, and you know what? That is ok too.

For some basis on what I mean, I will give you some examples of ways you can express and release your pent-up emotions. Walk outside and scream at the sky. Scream into a pillow. Heck, punch a pillow if you need to! Just don't direct that energy at your partner, and don't push it down so far inside you that you explode. Let it all out, and I promise you will feel better. Cry, scream, go on a walk, write it all down and throw it away, blaring heavy metal music, or vent it all out to your favorite stuffed animal. There are so many options there for you, and many that are unique and can only be discovered by you! The important thing is that you are comfortable and that your emotions get out there so you can process them. Anything you can do to prevent a negative fallout, without causing damage or harm to yourself or others, do it. It's ok. It's valid. It's natural. Whatever you do, if it makes you feel better, is perfectly validated. Just don't ignore those emotions, and don't hurt yourself or anyone else.

## Don't Speak or Act on Impulse.

Try to think through everything you do or say before you act on it. If you speak from raw emotion, your heart could be overruling your head. Give your brain a moment to catch up and process the emotions so you can piece together a response that will allow for open communication. You want to be able to address the issue with your partner while working together to resolve it. If you jump in with guns blazing, you probably won't get the results or the solution you need. This is the same with actions, regardless of the emotion or urge involved.

When you act on impulse, you also leap right over the boundaries, consent, expectations, trust, and respect that you have cultivated with your partner. This can lead to hurt, frustration, distrust, fear, and so much more. It is not fair to your partner to assume that what you want to do is ok, and just because you are angry, turned on, upset, sad, or experiencing any emotion and following your gut reactions does not make it right. Always take your partner into consideration before you do anything, and don't neglect the promises and expectations you have established together. That is a quick way to destroy any bond you have formed with your partner because you are dismissing the respect you have for your partner, and that can appear very inconsiderate.

Let me be clear here about what I mean regarding impulse. By impulse, I do not mean kissing your partner out of the blue, buying a gift that you just immediately know your partner will love or surprising your partner with something you know they will appreciate. I'm not talking about positive relationship instincts. What I mean by acting on impulse is crossing lines by acting on pure emotion without proper thought or consideration. For example, it is not considerate to say something mean out of anger without thinking, or to strike your partner out of anger, or to force your partner to do something just because you want to, right then, at that moment, regardless of their feelings. Don't let your emotions or desires overrule those of your partner, especially regarding the boundaries that you know for sure are set in stone. This can lead to serious, irreversible consequences.

Acting on impulse can lead to many misunderstandings, lots of confusion, heaps of hurt, a plethora of arguments, and so much more in a relationship. Take control of your impulses and strengthen both yourself and your relationship. Show your partner the trustworthiness and consideration they deserve. If you don't, your relationship will suffer, your partner may lose trust in you, and you will lose control over your own actions. Try to avoid this at all costs, unless you are absolutely sure it will not hurt your partner or relationship. When in doubt, speak up and ask your partner before doing or saying anything on impulse.

**Take Proper Care of Yourself**

Last but definitely not least, take care of yourself. Taking care of yourself is imperative for fostering healthy relationship communication, and it will prevent future conflicts. It is not selfish to take care of yourself, either. It is necessary! Eat nutritious meals, get enough sleep, and make sure you pay attention to your needs and emotions. All of these factor into your mood and wellbeing as a whole and this directly translates into your relationship. If you don't take care of yourself, you will feel grumpy, have low self-esteem, and much more. These negative factors can lead to frustration, which can bleed into your relationship and cause arguments, hurt, and misdirected anger.

Take care of yourself in order to take care of your relationship, and take care of your partner as well. All of these factor into a healthy relationship, healthy mindsets, and healthy bodies. If you and your partner are well taken care of, you will communicate and interact in a much more positive way!

# How to Pick Up the Pieces and Mend Bridges Together

Let's say you didn't listen to my advice about preventing an argument. Maybe you slipped up and need to find a way to reconcile your relationship. Whatever the reason, you are in the right place! Picking up the pieces after an argument is just as important as resolving the argument itself, and I am here to help you learn just how to do that. Let's go over some of the ways you can heal the wounds caused by arguments and become closer as a couple.

## Give Your Partner Space

Don't abandon your partner, but after an argument, you both need a little space and time. Give your partner, and yourself, that brief period where you can disconnect with the situation physically so that you can focus on it mentally. Simply go and sit in a separate room for a few minutes while your partner does the same. Cool down, reflect, and process what has occurred. This will give you both time to think things over and embrace forgiveness.

Take care when doing this, however. Do not blatantly ignore your partner if they seem as though they still need to talk, and make sure you make it clear that you are leaving the room so you can both calm down. If they think you are storming off in anger, giving the silent treatment, or ignoring the situation, it can give off the wrong impression and cause friction. Take all the space and time both of you need, but make it clear that you are doing it to cool off and process what has happened.

## Don't Resort to Make-Up Sex.

Going along with the above point, don't immediately fly into bed for make-up sex. That is never a good idea. Just as negative prods at your partner right after an argument are bad, positive distractions are bad too for similar reasons. If you leap back into intimacy right after an argument, it will distract your partner, and neither you nor they will be able to properly process their emotions. It will get thrown out the window in lieu of quick sexual gratification.

Additionally, having sex after an argument can feel a bit hollow, and it can start a pattern of sex for the sake of sex and take out the deeper intimacy and emotional connection that you need to be able to share in such an encounter. When you jump into make-up sex instead of healthy space and dialogue, it will take out an important communicative step as well, which is never a good idea. Your best bet is to wait a while, calm down, and don't mistake the heat of passion and anger for the urge to have sex.

## Learn from Your Mistakes and Apply it to the Future.

If you were the reason for the argument, and you've apologized sincerely, back up your words with actions. Make it your goal to do better next time and not repeat the action that caused the issue. Learn from your mistakes and grow as a person so your relationship will become stronger. Take every failure and turn it into a building block of knowledge that you can pour into the foundation of your relationship.

## Don't Beat Yourself Up About the Argument.

Everyone argues. It's natural, and at times it's good so you can get your thoughts and emotions out there. Having small conflicts actually builds the character of a relationship, so don't feel guilty if you have one with your partner. Just try to go over the steps I gave you for preventing further arguments, and you will be fine! Just make sure to sincerely apologize to your partner after a conflict, and make sure you let them know how much you appreciate them. Don't beat yourself up about it. It's ok!

## Don't Negate the Resolution of the Argument.

Once a conflict is resolved, leave it. Do not go back minutes or hours later, and try to re-justify what you said or did. This negates anything you have said before, and it breaks down the trust of the relationship. Once a conflict is resolved and done with, there is no need to go back and add extra bits of dialogue that will just flare it all back up again to cover your own behind. Leave the argument in the past, accept what you did wrong, and move on.

# CHAPTER 7
*Tips For Talking About Difficult Topics*

In any relationship, there are going to be some tough situations and difficult topics that are going to be brought up. These heavy conversations aren't often happily anticipated, but they are necessary. We're going to go over what these conversations could be, tips on how to handle and address them, and why we should not avoid these important but difficult conversations.

## Difficult Topics Many People Have to Face During Their Relationships

There is a wide variety of topics that people find difficult in their daily lives and relationships, and it is different for everyone. However, I'm going to highlight some of the most difficult roadblocks people come upon in their relationships so you can get an idea for the types of difficult topics I am referring to in my advice throughout this chapter. As I said, there are many more difficult topics that are not covered here, but the ones I've listed are ones that many people can relate to across the board.

### Loss

Loss of a loved one is likely the most difficult situation in anyone's life. Therefore, it can be very hard to talk about. The key here is to be absolutely considerate of your partner if they are going through loss and be there to support them. It can be difficult to know what to say in these situations, and sometimes silence is best, but try to let your partner know how much you care about them and that you are there whenever they need you. Discussing feelings after a loss can be really hard, but it is a big part of the overall healing process.

### Sexual Consent

Sexual consent is one of the more awkward topics we talk about in our relationships, but it is something we all must discuss for our own health, emotional wellbeing, and the stability of our relationships. Sexual consent conversations include but are not limited to: the use of protection and contraceptives, discussions about STI disclosure, the desire for whether or not to have children, the limits of sex positions, bondage, hard limits, exclusivity, and more. In order to have a good relationship, these discussions must take place for your safety and comfort in sexual situations.

## In-Laws

If you are married, in-laws are definitely going to come into the picture. This can be difficult at times, because you may feel like you are coming between your spouse and their family, or you may feel as though they are struggling to choose between you or their family. This power struggle between you and your spouse's family can put a big strain on your relationship, and discussing your anxieties about this may seem overwhelming. Don't fear your partner's reaction during these conversations and try to be as open and honest as you can be without pointedly attacking their family. It's a fine line that is hard to learn to walk, but if you discuss your in-laws with your spouse openly, it will turn out all right.

## Betrayal

We don't like to think it will happen to us, but betrayal can sometimes occur in a relationship. When this happens, your trust in your partner is fragile, you start questioning the relationship, and negative emotions start to stir. It can be really difficult to talk about this topic with your partner, because you may feel incredibly hurt and angry, but you have to if you want to mend the relationship. If your partner has betrayed your trust and you no longer wish to be with them, that is your call, but it is always a good idea to talk it out first and at least gain closure about the situation. Your emotions in this instant are entirely valid, but be the better person and hear what they have to say. You will probably feel better if you do.

## Money Problems

Money problems happen; it's just a natural speed bump in life. When they happen, however, you may feel stressed, embarrassed, and a number of other negative emotions. Instead of pushing those feelings away to hide your embarrassment from your partner, it is a good idea to reach out to them for support during that difficult time. They will likely be able to walk you through your issues and help you through your struggles. As a team, it's always best to work these things through together. Don't let your fear of embarrassment, tension, or argument keep you from being truthful about your finances or your feelings.

## Sickness and Other Health Issues

You may be embarrassed to talk about your health to your partner, but it is something you must do. If you hide your health issues from your partner, it will hurt your health, fracture the trust of the relationship, and make it impossible for your partner to help you through it and support you. I know sickness and health problems can be scary, but that is what your partner is there for! If you are in it for the long-run, you will want them to know what is ailing you so they can help you every step of the way. You are not a burden to them, and if they truly care, they are absolutely going to want to make sure you are ok above all else.

## Past Relationships

Ok, this is a big one. Most people do not want to bring up their past relationships because it can be very embarrassing, emotional, and awkward. It may also make your partner feel as though you are comparing them to an ex. Sometimes, however, it is important to discuss your past with your partner so that they will understand if certain insecurities pop up. If you discuss those insecurities with your partner, then if something makes you uncomfortable, they will know it is not because of them but because of a traumatic experience in your past. It will also help you both learn from past mistakes so you can strengthen your relationship and rise above the unhealthy ones from your past. Open up to your partner in the right way, and it will strengthen your bond. You can talk about past abusive relationships, distrustful ones, triggers, and the like, but here are some things that should be avoided for the health of your relationship: sex life, pet peeves, physical features, favorite date spots, songs that remind you of an ex, etc. It is good to talk about exes in some regards, just make sure to tread lightly and be smart about it.

# How to Handle Difficult Conversations

### Problem Solve and Tackle it Like a Team.

The most important tip I can give you is to handle difficult situations as a team. If you try to be right all the time or figure things out together, it can make your partner feel useless or like they are not a true part of the team. Work together to tackle these difficult topics so you can overcome things as a unit and grow together. It will strengthen your relational bonds, make it easier to tackle similar situations in the future and prevent your relationship from slowly fracturing over time. Remember, it's all about fixing the issue at hand and not one-upping your partner, especially in sensitive situations. Don't offer unwarranted advice or negate the comments that your partner makes. Instead, lean on one another and fight every battle as a team.

### Be Positive

It is very important to remain positive during a difficult situation. If you start making negative comments or retreating from an issue, it can cause stress, frustration, sadness, depression, and more that will cause the situation to spiral out of control. Take a deep breath, keep a level head, and try to be optimistic about the outcome of any situation you may have to face with your partner. In the end, if you want the situation to turn out ok, you have to believe that it will be so. Use compassion, smile, let yourself believe that things will get better, and lean on your partner. You can get through this; you just have to try! Express gratitude at the strength the both of you have for even bringing up the topic, and admire each other's courage. Thank one another for their courage, even. Pep yourself and your partner up and be strong, and you will know that you can tackle anything the world can throw at the two of you!

## Don't Put Your Walls Up.

Shutting down during difficult conversations and putting your walls up makes it very difficult for your partner to reach your level, understand what is going on, and help you tackle it. This can make it ten times harder to overcome adversity, and it is not healthy for you, your partner, or your relationship. Trust your partner and let your walls down. Express those emotions you are trying to hide and work through every situation together. You don't have to do this alone. That is what partnership is all about. You have to be trusting and vulnerable so you can navigate those difficult waters together. Be open and honest with these difficult subjects, and it will make all of the smaller things so much easier. If you can open up to your partner and get through the hardest relationship conversations together, you can do anything! What is there to fear?

## Utilize Empathy

Empathy and compassion are imperative during difficult situations. If things are rocky, it makes it a lot easier to navigate the situation if you are both open to seeing one another's perspectives and emotions so that you know how to tread carefully. Listen intently to your partner's words during difficult conversations, because you know it must have been hard for them to bring it up in the first place, and they care about you enough to open up and trust you with the situation. Understanding this concept is the first step to take. Then, make sure you give your full attention and remain invested throughout the entire conversation. Don't check out just because the conversation makes you uncomfortable or embarrassed. If your partner trusts you enough to bring the subject up, it is important enough for you to at least listen and offer support. Discuss the issue with your heart and lovingly find a solution together.

## Give it All the Time it Needs

Don't skimp and speed through difficult conversations just because it feels uncomfortable. This is degrading the importance of the topic, and it can make your partner feel that you are disinterested and uncaring of the situation. Additionally, choose the time for you to approach your partner wisely. Don't bombard your partner with it right as they walk through the door, just to get it out of the way. Choose a calm, stable time during which to discuss difficult topics to make sure that you are both on level ground. If you do it during an abrupt or busy time of day, the issue will not be resolved in a conclusive fashion, and you will be right back to square one. Make sure to discuss this with your partner, and ensure that you are both in a good enough place to start a conversation regarding the subject. Ask your partner "Is this a good time to talk?," "Can we discuss something that has been on my mind?", "Are you feeling well enough to discuss something important right now?" "I need some help. Do you have a minute for us to sit and talk?" and "When would you be comfortable discussing this issue?" to feel out the environment and pick the best time.

## Stay Focused on the Issue and Don't Divert from the Conversation.

The best thing to do during a difficult conversation is to stay on track. If you veer off during a difficult conversation, it won't get resolved when it needs to. It is best to resolve a difficult situation in one sitting so that it won't get brushed under the rug later on down the road. Embrace your courage and see each topic the whole way through to strengthen your relationship and your overall communication abilities. Stay on topic, and try to keep your partner on the same page as well. This will help you both grow in your dialogue and in your relationship. If your partner begins to get off-topic, gently nudge them back on track with phrases such as "That is a great point, but let's see if we can resolve this first. Then, we'll tackle our next step!", or "Let's handle one thing at a time so we can give it the attention it deserves!" These positive phrases will avoid the issue of your partner feeling unheard, and it will keep the current dialogue on track.

## Maintain Your Composure

It's easy to get a bit emotional during a difficult conversation, and that is understandable. However, don't let your emotions take control and get out of hand, or it can make it more difficult to talk about the situation. If you need to, you can take a small break and calm down, but don't let your emotions drive the path of the conversation. Try to remain calm and focus on the task at hand. Don't necessarily push away your emotions, because that can be dangerous, but don't let them overrule your mind while trying to resolve that is making you emotional. Additionally, try your best not to raise your voice or let yourself fall into a negative mindset. These can derail the dialogue and stimulate tension and aggression where it doesn't need to be. Talk yourself through these emotions, and express them to your partner so they can keep you on track. You can say, "I'm starting to feel a bit overwhelmed. Can you help me calm down for a few minutes, then we can get back on track? Thank you." This gives you both a moment to pause, collect yourselves, and continue in a constructive way.

## Go from Harder to Easier

When you attack a difficult subject, try to go at it from the top down to make it a much easier, fluid conversation. If you start out with the most upsetting or difficult part of a conversation, the rest will flow out much easier and get resolved much faster. Create a dialogue with your partner and think things through. Pinpoint the root cause of the issue, or the most difficult part, and discuss it with your partner. Use phrases such as, "Here is the issue. What do you think we should tackle first?" "What are you having the most trouble with regarding this subject?" "What is bothering you most about what we are about to discuss?" and "What scares you most about this topic?". By zeroing in on the hardest parts of a discussion, you can tackle it head-on as a team and knock it right out of the park! This makes the whole situation easier to resolve and less intimidating in the long-run.

## Remove Distractions

Make it harder for you and your partner to get off track by eliminating common distractions. Set your phones on silent mode, for instance, so the dialogue does not get derailed by a text message or phone call. You can always respond to them later, but your relationship is more important at this time. Turn off the television, so you don't veer off into a seemingly easier environment. Turn the radio off as music can alter the ambiance of a room. Make every effort you can to focus on the task at hand and highlight its importance to you and your partner.

## Don't Deflect or Minimize Your Partner's Emotions.

Your emotions, as well as your partner's, are valid and justified in every way during a conversation. The worst thing you can do is deflect away from these emotions. Validate your partner's emotions and tackle the root of their cause so you will both feel better after a conversation. Deflecting these emotions can make your partner feel sad, unimportant, and uncared for. This is the opposite of what should occur during a situation because you both want to remain as positive as you can during difficult times. Avoid, at all costs, phrases such as "Grow up," "Everyone feels that way, what makes you any different?" "You'll get over it," "You're dragging me down," "Just ignore it," "Feel this way instead," "Stop being so upset!" and "It's silly to feel that way." These phrases can damage the self-esteem and emotional stability of your partner, so it is best not to say them at all during a sensitive conversation. Instead, be your partner's shoulder to cry on, their rock, and their confidant. Let them know that you hear them, you understand their pain, and that you are there to help in any way that you can.

**Don't Give Direct Advice, but Phrase it as a Question.**

Instead of telling your partner what to do, when there is no way you know exactly how they are feeling or handling a situation, suggest resolutions in the form of a question. For instance, say: "Would it help if you did this?" instead of "You should do this because I know it will be the best solution," or "This is what you need to do." Other beneficial phrases include: "Do you want to try this together to see if it helps?" "Would you mind if I suggest a possible solution?" "How would you feel if we tried it this way?" "Can I give you a few possible choices, and we can choose one together to see if it works?" and "Would you like to try this with me and see if it helps?" Phrasing things as a question is a great way to offer advice while giving your partner the power to choose instead of feeling like they aren't good enough to choose for themselves how to handle their emotions. If you tell them what to do in an emotional situation, it could just backfire and make those emotions flare. In any situation, it is best to ask your partner how they feel about something before suggesting that they try it for themselves.

# Why You Should Not Avoid Difficult Conversations

When there is a difficult discussion that must be bad, don't ignore it. Pushing the topic away is the most detrimental thing you can do in your relationship. By tackling the most difficult discussions together, your relationship will grow and blossom and strengthen so much. Don't let yourself be overruled by anxiety or uncomfortable feelings, because it may cause you to avoid the situation entirely if you get too scared. Acknowledge that those emotions are there, and move toward a solution to remedy them. Here's a hint: The solution to fixing those emotions is to talk through the difficult situation and find a solution.

If you avoid a difficult conversation, you will ultimately stunt the growth of your entire relationship. If you can't get past things that try to bring your relationship and emotions down, how are you going to grow moving forward? You have to get the problems out of the way in a conducive manner in order to truly move on with your relationship. Basically, avoiding difficult subjects is like putting a roadblock right under the tires of your relationship. It can't move forward if you don't get that roadblock out of the way, and moving backward is not something you want to do.

The bottom line is that if you don't face your difficult topics, they will remain difficult forever and just get worse with time. Don't avoid important things just because they are hard. Life is hard, but you have made it this far, and you should be proud of that. Take that pride and channel it into your conversations. Nothing is too big for you and your partner to handle. Your relationship is stronger than any challenge you will face, and if you believe that, you will both go far!

Look, I know it's scary. These conversations are scary, but you are stronger than this! Your relationship deserves that strength and courage, and your partner deserves it, too. Be the rock that your relationship can stand on, and initiate the conversations that must be had to move forward in your relationship. Tackling difficult conversations has a very good impact on your relationship, so fight them head-on! Don't short-circuit your relationship and unravel all of the progress you've made so far. Push past the grudges of difficult topics, and you will come out swinging. Your partner, and your relationship, will thank you. I promise!

# CHAPTER 8
## *The Languages Of Love*

The key to proper relationship communication is knowing how your partner expresses and receives love. This is a very strong communication of feelings, and it is a great indicator of how your partner can feel special. How we feel and express love is very closely linked to how we communicate and show affection in a relationship. These languages of love express the venues through which each individual feels, gives, and expresses love in their own way. Some people are entirely affiliated with one of these, and some are linked to many. Each person is unique, and the way they feel and express love is unique, too. You can love intimacy while feeling appreciated through acts of service, or you could simply feel love through the giving and receiving of gifts alone. Let's go over each of these love languages to see how love is communicated in each way, and which one may be calling out to you!

## Physical Touch and Intimacy

Physical touch is what it sounds like. The love language of physical touch involves expressing or receiving your love in the form of skin-to-skin contact or general physical proximity where you can touch one another. It is a very passionate love language, and it is very common in those who have a very deep physical bond with their partner. It's also common in newlyweds, but it can be found in any walk of the relationship journey. Examples of physical touch include:

- Hugging
- Kissing
- Holding hands
- Sexual intimacy
- Massage
- Cuddling
- Pats on the head
- Placing a comforting hand on your partner's shoulder
- Leaning against your partner while sitting next to one another
- Playing footsies
- Sitting on your partner's lap.
- Gentle biting
- Rubbing or scratching your partner's back

Now, let's talk about how we can use physical touch to communicate love into your relationship! Remember how we talked about physical communication? This is the love child of physical communication! You can easily express your love and affection every day by using physical communication. When your partner is down in the dumps, placing a gentle hand on their shoulder can be enough to show that you care! When you are sad, your partner can express their understanding and love for you by giving you a tight, warm hug that translates so well into feelings of security, support, affection, and connectivity.

If you're feeling frisky, what better way to communicate it than physical touch? When you get hot and bothered, save the words for later and pepper your sweet partner with kisses and stimulating caresses. If you are feeling happy, hugs, and swinging your intertwined hands while you walk, communicate that very clearly. If you are stressed, there is no better way for your partner to love you than to give you a calm, relaxing massage to show that they care. See how easy it is to express your love and emotions with physical touch? It plays very well in our discussion on relationship communication, and it is a great way to feel close to your partner.

## Quality Time Together

Quality time has a lot to do with simply knowing that your partner is there, in close proximity, and you revel in the presence of one another, whether or not you touch, talk, or interact, though those are a plus. People who respond to quality time like to plan movie nights, special dates, and game nights in order to woo their partners, and they normally feel the most connection when their partner does the same.

Examples of quality time include:
- Going on a dinner date
- Watching a movie together
- Planting a garden together
- Going on a walk together
- Visiting new and exciting places together
- Tackling obstacles as a team
- Playing games together
- Exercising with one another
- Playing a competitive video game together.
- Learning how to do something new together
- Finding new hobbies together, such as taking up an instrument, making pottery, rock climbing, archery, or cooking
- Build something together, such as a birdhouse or a bench
- Going on a drive together
- Doing everyday tasks together, such as cooking together or folding clothes together.
- Being in the same room, even if not talking, such as sitting next to each other and reading.

Now, how can we use the quality time to incorporate affection into our relationship communication? I'll show you how! Nonverbal communication is just as important in relationship communication as any other form. Quality time is where that comes into play. Choosing to be in the same room as your partner is its own unique form of communication. It communicates closeness, the security of being near one you love, and the message that you are not ignoring them. It makes your partner feel special, and it makes you happy just knowing that they are nearby.

If you or your partner are attuned to this love language, it is important to be able to pick up on their stance in the relationship. For instance, if you know that your partner shows affection by being near you, and they withhold that affection by staying distance, there may be something wrong. Reach out to them and ask why they don't feel as secure or loved in your presence to figure out why their expression of affection may have shifted. It may seem subtle at first, but if you truly understand your partner, you will be able to pick up on this.

Alternatively, if your partner spends more time around you than before, then you know your relationship is doing ok and that things are happy and full of love! If you and your partner enjoy quality time as your form of love, express it openly by spending as much time together as you can!

## Sincere Words of Affirmation

Words of affirmation are popular for those who like to have stability and reliance on their partner in order to feel loved and appreciated. Being told thank you, I love you, and you look beautiful, etc. are incredibly uplifting for individuals who have an affinity to this love language. They are also often the first to give praise and to glow and smile upon receiving it.

Examples of words of affirmation include:
- Detailed compliments
- Saying thank you
- Telling your partner that you appreciate them and what they do
- Saying I love you
- Laughing at your partner's jokes
- Expressing that you are proud of your partner
- Cheering your partner on
- Letting your partner know you are there
- Telling your partner that they are safe in scary situations
- Leaving your partner cute love notes throughout the house
- Sending your partner sweet text messages, voice mails, emojis, and emails
- Saying you admire your partner or a certain quality of your partner

The love language of words of affirmation is probably the easiest love language you can utilize in your relationship communication. We communicate with words, after all! Use your love language to shower your partner with words of appreciation, and they will do the same back to you! Communicate everything in your heart openly and honestly, and you won't go wrong.

If you are down, your partner can cheer you up by expressing their love for you in words and saying how proud they are of you. If you are happy, your partner can rejoice right along with you and uplift your spirits even more! If you are scared, your partner can sit next to you and whisper in your ear that they are there, they will protect you, and that there is nothing to fear. The reassurance of words is the strongest way to make someone feel loved if they are attuned to words of affirmation. Use that to strengthen your relationship and sew affection into the dialogue you have with your partner.

# Affectionate Gift Giving

Gift-giving can show up in many forms, but it involves the giving and receiving of items, handmade presents, and other forms of loving gifts. They are often quite crafty, either with creating items or cooking and show off their affections by communicating love by giving the things they make or buy to their loved ones. They also adore being surprised with little gifts, regardless of the value, and appreciate the thought of being remembered on special occasions.

Examples of gift-giving include:

- Making something by hand for your partner
- Buying your partner something they need, such as a new jacket, pair of shoes, or phone case
- Remembering your partner on their birthday with a thoughtful present
- Showering your partner with gifts during Christmas or similar holidays
- Creating a photo album of all of the memories you and your partner share
- Painting a mural or picture for your partner
- Buying your partner something useful or related to one of their hobbies, such as a new blender for someone who likes to cook or a vacuum for someone who likes to clean
- Buying new, comfortable pillows for the bed when you notice that your partner is having trouble sleeping at night
- Surprising your partner with a heartfelt gift, or something you know your partner wants
- Surprising your partner with their favorite meal or treat

Gift giving is a sweet way to communicate love in our relationships, and it is easy because there are so many ways that we can do it! You can give your partner a special gift on their birthday to communicate that you remembered. You can give your partner a sweet bouquet of flowers to tell them that you love them. You can bring them their favorite foods when they are sad to cheer them up and communicate that you care. You can bring them a giant teddy bear to snuggle when they are scared or sick. Communicate the effort you want to put into the relationship by making your partner a handmade present! You can even show a sign that you would like to get intimate by gifting your partner a new toy for the bedroom if you are into that kind of thing. All of these ways communicate your love in different ways, and there are many more! Get creative and find new ways to show your affection through gift-giving. It can be really fun!

Communicate your love by giving gifts on special occasions instead of simply speaking to acknowledge their importance. This makes the occasion feel more validated, and the gift feels more from the heart. Take some time to get to know your partner and figure out the kinds of things that they like, and you will open the door to many new possibilities in your relationship!

## Devoted Acts of Service/Kindness

Acts of service are closely linked to the heart because when you do something for someone you love, it shows that you truly care for them and want to help out as much as you can. Doing something for someone you love can bring you so much joy if it is the way that you express and receive love, and it can be expressed in many different ways. People with this love language will often ask what they can do for their partner throughout the day to make it easier or more enjoyable for them. They show their love in every way through taking some time to take a load off for the other person. This can be small, simple tasks or large, extravagant ones. Each sign of affection holds its own message, and it can vary based on the level of affection you have for an individual, specific days or situations, and more!

Examples of acts of service/kindness include:
- Cooking your partner's favorite meal
- Bandaging a wound for your partner
- Driving your partner to an important meeting
- Bringing home your partner's favorite meal
- Surprising your partner by washing their car
- Repairing a broken item of your partner's
- Giving your partner a soothing massage
- Cleaning for your partner after a long day
- Making the bed
- Running to the store for your partner.
- Helping your partner finish a difficult task

Incorporate acts of service into your relationship dialogue easily by expressing care for your partner. If your partner is feeling stressed or overwhelmed from the day's work, show that you care by cleaning up some dishes or finishing a task for your partner that they were too busy to do. Show your partner your deepest love by helping them out when they are burdened. Take a weight off their shoulders and give them the support they need to show your deepest devotion and love.

Communicate compassion by cooking your partner a bowl of homemade soup when they are sick. If your partner is worried or frustrated about something, fix it. If they are sad, do something to make them happy. If they are tired, make them a nice cup of coffee or give them some time to take a nap. If they are feeling frisky, and you are too, show an act of service by initiating a steamy sexual encounter, complete with foreplay and lots of bodily kisses. There are so many ways to communicate acts of kindness into your relationship, specific to situations you feel need to be acted upon. You just have to find the right act to meet the situation, and the possibilities can be endless!

## The Languages of Love Quiz

Now that we know what the languages of love are let's take a fun little quiz to see which one (or ones) you are most attuned to! That way, you will know how to communicate with your partner how you can feel the most loved and appreciated. Then, your partner can take it too so you can know how to shower them with love in a way that makes them happiest! Once you know your love language, you open up a whole world of possibilities for you and your relationship communication going forward. I hope you've enjoyed all of the advice I've given you so far!

For each statement, give a numerical value between one and five to indicate how much it speaks to you. In the end, tally up your totals based on the letter associated with each question to find out which love language is strongest for you! For instance, tally up your totals for each statement labeled P, Q, and so forth, and compare your totals for each letter.

1. P: I love to be kissed by my partner in order to feel cared for. _
2. Q: I enjoy watching a late-night movie with my partner, regardless of our distance to one another. _
3. G: I like receiving handmade gifts from my partner because it makes me feel appreciated. _
4. S: I like it when my partner helps me tackle a difficult task because it shows that they care. _
5. W: I love hearing sweet nothings whispered into my ear. _
6. P: I like to hold hands with my partner in public to feel that they want to be near to me physically at times. _
7. Q: I like to go on adventurous trips with my partner. _

8. G: I love receiving thoughtful surprises from my partner, such as a piece of clothing or jewelry that I have been eyeing. _
9. S: I like it when my partner opens the door for me. It makes me feel special. _
10. W: I love hearing phrases such as "I am proud of you," and "I appreciate you." _
11. P: I like receiving massages from my partner and feeling their hands on me. _
12. Q: I like to sit and eat dinner together with my partner. _
13. G: I love to receive thoughtful knick knacks from my partner to remind me of our relationship and how much it has meant to us. _
14. S: I enjoy coming home to a house cleaned by my partner after a long day. _
15. W: I like it when my partner sends me cute messages and emojis throughout the day to feel appreciated. _
16. P: I like to snuggle with my partner when we are in a room together. _
17. Q: I enjoy simply sitting in the same room as my partner, regardless of what we are doing. _
18. G: I enjoy it when my partner remembers me on special occasions by giving me gifts. _
19. S: It makes me feel good when my partner does little tasks for me throughout the day. _
20. W: I like hearing the words "I love you" more than the physical signs of love. _
21. P: I enjoy it when my partner touches me spontaneously throughout the day, such as with a quick hug, a kiss on the head, or a gentle caress. _
22. Q: I like to run daily errands with my partner just to be near to them. _
23. G: I like being surprised with sweets and/or my favorite foods by my partner. _
24. S: I enjoy it when my partner draws me a warm bath or makes the bed for me. _
25. W: I love being listened to after a particularly emotional day, and being told that everything is ok. _
26. P: I like to be comforted by a hug rather than words. _
27. Q: I feel comforted and safe most by the calming presence of my partner. _
28. G: When my partner gives me something, it makes me feel appreciated, and it gives our relationship security. _
29. S: When my partner does something to fix an issue for me, it makes me feel better. _

30. W: When someone tells me that everything is going to be ok, it means more than if someone were to give me a hug or try to fix it themselves. _
31. P: I get turned on by physical touch. _
32. Q: The presence of my partner gets me hot and bothered. _
33. G: Receiving a sexy gift from my partner gets me in the mood. _
34. S: When my partner gives me a back rub or makes me feel pampered, it makes me feel very romantic. _
35. W: I get stimulated very easily when my partner whispers steamy words into my ear. _
36. P: When I am feeling sad, I just want to be held. _
37. Q: When I am upset, I just want to be around my partner. _
38. G: When I am sad, gifts cheer me up more than anything. _
39. S: When I am not feeling happy, it makes me feel better when my partner does something thoughtful for me. _
40. W: When I am upset, my partner can cheer me up easily with kind words. _
41. P: I get excited about the future with my partner when we hold hands. _
42. Q: I can envision a life with my partner when we spend time together. _
43. G: I feel like my partner will be able to provide for me if I receive gifts. _
44. S: I can see myself marrying a partner who accomplishes tasks for me and helps me around the house. _
45. W: I love discussing the future with my partner. _
46. P: When I am feeling lonely, I want my partner to touch me to let me know that they are there. _
47. Q: When I am feeling lonely, all it takes is for my partner to step into the room to feel better. _
48. G: When I am lonely, it makes me feel better to receive a special gift from my partner. _
49. S: When I am feeling lonely, I like it when my partner drives me around. _
50. W: When I am feeling lonely, all I need to hear is that my partner is there for me. _

**Here is how you scored:**
If you tallied most for P, you are most likely attuned to *physical touch*.
If you tallied most for Q, you are most likely attuned to *quality time*.
If you tallied most for G, you are most likely attuned to *gift-giving*.
If you tallied most for S, you are most likely attuned to *acts of service*.
If you tallied most for W, you are most likely attuned to *words of affirmation*.

# CONCLUSION

Thank you for reading *Relationship Communication*. I truly hope that it has given you ample insight into your relationship and the communication involved to keep it healthy and long-lasting! I also hope that it has been in at least a small way enlightening for your journey ahead as you traverse the waters of your relationship. As we know, those waters can be rocky, but through the guides in this book, I'm sure you can cross those waves with ease and come out floating on the waters of a healthy relationship! As I stated at the beginning of this book, my mission is to help you and your partner form deep bonds full of trust and open, honest communication. I hope I have achieved the goal of showing you how to reach those deep bonds and how to tackle any relationship endeavor that is tossed your way, through proper communication! If you have a stable, honest, and true relationship, you are on the right track! Just stay open, caring, empathetic, and smart about it, and you won't go wrong! Keep this book handy, if you want, in case you lose track along the way!

Alright, let's have a recap. In this book, we covered, over the course of the many detailed chapters and subchapters, the topics pertaining to relationship communication. These included the definition of relationship communication, what that means to you, and how you can use that communication in your personal relationships through various means. These means include physical touch, verbal communication, signing, body language, written words, and more! We then moved on to tackling the monster that is conflict resolution. We also found out many ways that we can fight that conflict head-on without attacking our partner!

After we accomplished that, we went on to discussing common relationship mishaps, including staying silent, suppressing emotions, being too much of a crutch, and jumping to conclusions. Whew, that was a lot! But we did it! We also found out how to tackle those mishaps so they don't stand in the way of the best relationship we can achieve in a healthy manner.

Then we got into the soft and mushy, but endearing, subject of empathy. We talked about how tuning into your partner's emotions, while not necessarily feeding off of them, can lead to a closer bond and a greater safety net of trust between the two of you. Then, we got steamy! We talked about communication's passionate and closely intertwined connection to intimacy in the bedroom. Finally, we talked about how to tackle difficult topics, and we also learned what the five languages of love are and how to express them!

The next step that I would recommend going forward is to follow the practices laid out in this book and to avoid the red flags I brought up as well. I hope that you can carry this through your relationship as an aid so that your relationships may blossom!

If you found this book helpful and worth your time, please leave a kind and honest review on Amazon. I always appreciate the sincere feedback so that I may improve upon my books over time. I also love to see what people think about my book and how it has helped them! Thank you again for choosing my book out of the many that circulate on the market today. I hope that it was worth your time!

# DESCRIPTION

Would you like to grow closer to your partner? Are your relationships suffering from a lack of communication, pent up frustration, a plethora of misunderstandings, apparent disinterest, or other negative factors? What you need are proper communication skills! Relationship communication is incredibly important for strengthening your relational bonds, mending bridges, growing closer intimately, expressing emotions, preventing arguments, and so many other areas of a relationship. I'm here to help you unravel the complicated web of dialogue in a relationship, and I want to show you how you can apply communication skills in every possible aspect of your relationship so that it can bloom, strengthen, and grow in a healthy way. This book can lead you down a wonderful path in your relationship, and it can help you jump through the many hoops and hurdles that partnership brings to the table.

Topics I will bring to light in this book, and key points I will be addressing include:

- How to resolve conflicts
- How to prevent conflicts from occurring
- How to mend the damage caused by arguments and misunderstandings
- How to strengthen intimacy with verbal and bodily communication
- How to communicate your intimate needs and wants with touch, sound, and sight
- What it means to address consent, expectations, and hang-ups
- How to identify and utilize the five languages of love
- What relationship communication really means
- What relationship communication specifically means to you.
- The many outlets for communication, including physical, verbal, and more!
- Tackling common relationship mishaps
- Learning how to tackle and discuss difficult topics
- How to embrace and understand empathy
- And finally, how to talk to your partner!

Let this book be a guiding light that shines into your relationship and illuminates all of the wonderous opportunities available to you both. Let that revelation lead you down a path to growth, happiness, and love! With this book by your side, you can tackle anything that comes your way in your relationship, and you can resolve it with thoughtful, mature conversations. You will find that these conversations, and the methods you will learn in this book, are not as complicated as they may seem! You just have to learn how to navigate them, and this book will show you the way! Leaf through these chapters and open your eyes to a world of possibilities in your relationship!

Learn to let your walls down so you can open up to your partner, find out how trust and respect can become the glue that holds you two together, and express yourself in ways you never knew you could. You can do all of this, and more if you let yourself figure out how. I will show you how to understand and express all that is needed in a healthy and strong relationship if you will let me. All you have to do is allow yourself to be willing and receptive to the truth behind relationships and the honest communication involved. I know you can do it, and your partner will thank you for it!

www.ingramcontent.com/pod-product-compliance
Lightning Source LLC
Chambersburg PA
CBHW060257030426
42335CB00014B/1737